New Mexico

Voices in an Ancient Landscape

BOOKS BY DOUGLAS KENT HALL

Rock:
A World Bold As Love

On the Way to the Sky

Let 'Er Buck!

Rock and Roll Retreat Blues

Rodeo

Ski with Billy Kidd

The Master of Oakwindsor

Van People:
The Great American
Rainbow Boogie

Arnold:
The Education of a Bodybuilder
(with Arnold Schwarzenegger)

Bodyshaping for Women
(with Arnold Schwarzenegger)

Bodymagic (with Lisa Lyon)

The Incredible Lou Ferrigno

Working Cowboys

The Border:
Life on the Line

In Prison

Passing Through:
Meditations on the West

Frontier Spirit:
Churches of the Southwest

New Mexico:
Voices in an Ancient Landscape

New Mexico

Voices in an Ancient Landscape

Douglas Kent Hall

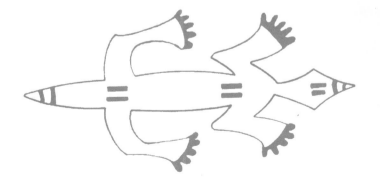

A JOHN MACRAE BOOK

Henry Holt and Company

New York

Henry Holt and Company, Inc.
Publishers since 1866
115 West 18th Street
New York, New York 10011

Henry Holt® is a registered trademark of
Henry Holt and Company, Inc.

Published in Canada by Fitzhenry & Whiteside Ltd.,
195 Allstate Parkway, Markham, Ontario L3R 4T8.

Library of Congress Cataloging-in-Publication Data
Hall, Douglas Kent.
New Mexico: voices in an ancient landscape/
Douglas Kent Hall. — 1st ed.
p.   cm.
"A John Macrae book."
1. Espanola Valley (N.M.) — History.   2. Espanola
Valley (N.M.) — Description and travel.   I. Title.
F802.E8H35   1995   94-42888
978.9'52 — dc20   CIP

ISBN 0-8050-1233-8

Henry Holt books are available for special promotions
and premiums. For details contact:
Director, Special Markets.

First Edition — 1995

Designed by Lucy Albanese

Printed in the United States of America
All first editions are printed on acid-free paper. ∞

10 9 8 7 6 5 4 3 2 1

Front matter illustrations: *page iii: Deathhead Palma,
Los Matachines de Alcalde; page vi: Pueblo Singers; page
xiii: Morada; page xvi: Sikh Leader, Somrillo; page xvii:
Malinche and Dancers, Los Matachines de Alcalde;
page xviii: Capilla de San Miguel, Ranchitos; page xix:
Dog Walking*

To dawn and devon

Contents

New Mexico

Voices in an
Ancient Landscape

In the center and middle, then, of North America there lies the region or peninsula of New Spain, where the discovery of New Mexico has been made. It lies more than twelve hundred miles northward from Old Mexico, and six hundred of these are desert, inhabited by innumerable Indians so barbarous and savage that they are naked and have no houses or agriculture, supporting themselves on all kinds of animals, which they hunt and eat raw, as will be told in the proper place. But, upon reaching the settlements of New Mexico, there are people who wear clothes and shoes and who are excellent farmers.

FRAY ALONZO DE BENAVIDES

BLACK MESA

Discovery and Conquest

*Every man contains within himself a ghost continent —
a place circled as warily as Antarctica was circled two
hundred years ago by Captain Cook.*

LOREN EISELEY

This could easily be fiction. Or fantasy. So pure was the experience of giving oneself up to northern New Mexico. I remember driving along the Rio Grande first as a teenager, in a time when the road held closer to the river; even then I was touched by the land's spare and magical beauty. Memories of New Mexico stayed with me through the years. I returned to spend vacations, learning the land, watching dances on dirt plazas shimmering with dry summer heat, drinking cold beer in Evangelo's in Santa Fe, eating chile in village restaurants up and down the Rio Grande. Later, when I began seeking a new place to live, images of New Mexican landscapes with cottonwood *bosques* and low hills unfolding to a dramatic horizon and a vast sky brought me back. Aside from answering to its subtle mysteries and being caught up in its history I had little reason to be here.

For centuries people have responded unreasonably to this high desert island that rises between the austere depths of the Grand Canyon and the windswept plateau we now know as the Texas Panhandle. New Mexico attracted adventurers and exploiters, men primarily interested in adding to their fortunes. So intent were they on bringing the Christian religion to the indigenous people and claiming the country's fabled wealth that the first Europeans accepted almost without question the absurd and paradoxical tales that promised a new land even richer than the prosperous mining regions of Mexico.

The stories that fed the greed of the conquistadors and finally coaxed them north into the territory of New Mexico issued from the same order of avarice that had fueled the colonizing of old Mexico, Guatemala, and the countries of South America — promises of gold and silver and the glory and adventure that went with their attainment. The desire for wealth aroused passions and enlivened imaginations. It caused men like Álvar Núñez Cabeza de Vaca to describe in elaborate detail treasures he'd never seen.

Cabeza de Vaca was a sailor who had survived a shipwreck during the Narváez expedition from Cuba along the coast of the Gulf of Mexico in 1528. In the company of three companions, including a Moorish slave, he spent the next eight years adrift, wandering the breadth of the land that would become Texas. They encountered Indians, learned from them, and lived among them, often at their mercy. From these experiences Cabeza de Vaca pieced together tales that hinted at great wealth in the lands to the north. They formed the substance of the report he delivered to Antonio de Mendoza, the first viceroy of New Spain.

Cabeza de Vaca's apochryphal tales were repeated and amplified by other unreliable reporters, and his words were embellished by Fray Marcos de Niza, the distinguished Father Provincial of the Franciscan Order. The false words provided impetus for Marcos's own ill-fated foray into Zuni country in 1539.

Fray Marcos's adventures read like a chapter out of a child's storybook. In addition to the friar's notoriety as a theologian and cosmographer, he was also a seasoned explorer who had traveled in Guatemala and in Peru with Pizarro. Such learning and experience should have afforded him a better perspective on his slender chances for a successful mission to the north. Even Marcos's choice of Estevan, the legendary black slave who had gained a reputation as a medicine man and guide while traveling with Cabeza de Vaca, seems to indicate a lapse in judgment. The magnitude of the Mexican discoveries was so great, from the earliest gold treasures of Cortés, the weight of which could be measured in tons, to the massive silver lode found in Zacatecas in 1548, that the incautious Spaniards had learned to credit stories of bonanza strikes.

Francisco de Ibarra, who had opened mines in Zacatecas, went on to discover the mines at San Martín, then Nombre de Dios, and Durango—evidence enough that each step northward might hold its reward. Like the others before them, Fray Marcos and Mendoza read those successes as evidence that wealth in the New World was almost without end and that to obtain it one had merely to travel northward into unexplored territories to lay claim to it.

In the early months of 1539, Fray Marcos, with the full support of Francisco Vásquez de Coronado, the newly appointed governor of New Galicia, set off to find what fable had labeled the Seven Cities of Cibola, a cluster of settlements rumored to have been founded by the Seven Bishops of Portugal. These churchmen, said to have fled Iberia in A.D. 714, in the midst of the upheaval and outrage of the Moorish invasion, had purportedly set up a stronghold in the New World that was filled with amazing treasure and governed by utopian theory. It was a naive and fanciful notion, but like almost every other story glorifying the vast unexplored continent of North America, it fed an imagination that had already been witness to wealth.

Fray Marcos led his main party into what would become New Mexico. Estevan, dressed in the bright colors of a court jester, carrying a "magic" gourd he'd been given on the long trek with Cabeza de Vaca, his body hung with tiny bells, pressed on northward, ahead of the main procession. Flanked by two greyhounds and accompanied by a number of faithful Indians, the black slave scouted each new village for signs of gold and then marked his path with a series of white crosses, his signal to Fray Marcos.

The priest followed the trail of crosses, his own optimism steadily growing, until one day with no warning he encountered three terrified runners who had escaped from the Zuni Indians. They brought news that Estevan had made it to the Zuni village of Hawikuh; however, there was no word of treasure. Estevan and many of the Indians with him had been set upon, captured, and savagely murdered by the people of the village.

Shaken, Fray Marcos continued to advance cautiously until he glimpsed, from a distant rise, the village where the former slave had met his death. In his report, Fray

Marcos described it as a "beautiful city" and went on to say that it was "bigger than the city of Mexico." He admitted to being in a quandary: "At times I was tempted to go to it, because I knew I risked nothing but my life, which I had offered to God the day I commenced the journey; finally I feared to do so, considering my danger and that if I died, I would not be able to give an account of this country."

To claim the region for the Spanish crown, Fray Marcos hastily planted a spindly cross in a pile of stones, and then, fearing that the Zunis would come out to kill him, too, he fled back to Mexico.

Fray Marcos's claim to have seen one of the Seven Cities of Cibola went unchallenged; it was esteemed important enough, in fact, to justify organizing a more comprehensive expedition under Coronado, who led a force of three hundred men deep into the country north from Mexico. In the following year, 1540, Hernando de Soto was also pushing hard into the interior of North America from the east, on his way to the Mississippi River, which he would "discover" only weeks before Native Americans would dump his body into the river's delta without ceremony. Luck was beginning to run its course for Spain in America.

Coronado, a soldier of good reputation who had married well and made his way successfully into politics, was possessed of the stature necessary to undertake the mission. His search was comprehensive, extending as far west as the coast of Mexico and as far north and east as the Texas Panhandle, Oklahoma, and Kansas. The expedition's costs were staggering.

Like his predecessors, Coronado found no great hoards of treasure, but his optimism ran high, as one can read from a fragment of his letter back to Mendoza, the viceroy: "I send you samples of the weapons with which the natives of this country fight—a shield, a hammer, and a box with some arrows, among which are two with bone points, the like of which have never been seen, according to what these conquerors say. As far as I can judge, it does not appear to me that there is any hope of getting gold or silver, but I trust in God that if there is any we shall get our share of it and it shall not escape us through any lack of diligence in the search."

Among his expedition's discoveries were the Colorado River and the Grand Canyon.

SWORD MASTER/ARTIST, OJO CALIENTE

He observed vast herds of buffalo. He encountered nomadic tribes and native people living in pueblos. He also located bare traces of minerals, but none of the great wealth alleged to have been cached in the Seven Cities of Cibola or anyplace else.

Coronado was methodical. His quest was as thorough as his resources, both physical and financial, would permit. In order to follow up every lead suggested by Fray Marcos and others, he divided his men into small groups, assigned them to an officer, and dispatched them in different directions. He sent Captain Francisco de Barrionuevo's group north to explore the provinces of the Jemez and to the Tewa in the Espanola Valley. Their findings are recorded by Pedro de Castañeda, a common soldier whose remarkable account of the expedition is among the most authoritative of the early writings about frontier America: "Captain Francisco de Barrionuevo was sent up the river toward the north with several men. He saw two provinces, one of which was called Hemes and had seven villages, and the other Yunqueyunque. The inhabitants of Hemes came out peaceably and furnished provisions. At Yunqueyunque the whole nation left two very fine villages which they had on either side of the river entirely vacant, and went into the mountains, where they had four very strong villages in a rough country, where it was impossible for horses to go. In the two villages there was a great deal of food and some very beautiful glazed earthenware with many figures and different shapes. Here they also found many bowls full of a carefully selected shining metal with which they glazed the earthenware. This shows that mines of silver would be found in that country if they should hunt for them."

The Coronado expedition bore all the perils of sixteenth-century exploration. His soldiers experienced hunger, encountered hostile natives, and suffered the effects of hard travel in a treacherous and unforgiving terrain. Coronado himself was not spared. He rode at the head of his party, constantly in the face of danger. During one battle two valiant captains came to his aid, shielding his body with their own, and his life was spared.

Later, on a feast day, while he was out riding one of his powerful mounts in a race against Don Rodrigo Maldonado, the girth on Coronado's saddle broke. He fell and Maldonado's horse catapulted over him, striking his head with its hooves and leaving him near death. He recovered slowly and finally suffered being transported back to Mexico on a litter, carrying with him nothing of substance to offset his two-and-a-half-year exploration.

Coronado filed a disappointing report, which included the distressing news that over half of his men had perished during the expedition. With that, the dream of riches should then have been forgotten forever. Typically, only the report was forgotten.

Forty years later, with another generation in control and eager to duplicate the good fortune of their forebears in Mexico and Peru, the Spaniards once again ventured northward. New names were added to the roster of adventurers and religious men who sought to conquer the land. There were men with good and honorable intentions as well as men blinded by pettiness and greed. Their names were Tovar, Antonio de Espejo, Gaspar Castano de Sosa, Francisco Leybe de Bonilla, and Antonio Gutiérrez de Humana, and they accomplished no more than those who had gone before.

Spanish laws of colonization promulgated in 1573 required that any colonizing expedition had to be authorized by the viceroy. These permits were not easily obtained, and some individuals grew impatient for permission and bypassed the law. Gaspar Castano de Sosa, the chief magistrate of San Luis, Nuevo León, set out on July 27, 1590, to colonize New Mexico without authorization. His group of more than 160 men traveled as far as Santo Domingo Pueblo on the Rio Grande before he was arrested by Captain Juan de Morlete and taken back to face Viceroy Luis de Velasco.

Notable among the authorized expeditions, if only for its sheer bravado, was one mounted by Fray Agustín Rodríguez, a lay Franciscan brother whose intention was to carry the message of Christ to the native people.

Like most of the priests in the New World, Fray Rodríguez had a genuine passion to save the souls of the natives. Hundreds of his fellow priests labored among the tribes of Mexico with genuine fervor; they saw it as both duty and calling. An example of that well-meant intent is clearly set forth in the writings of Fray Antonio de la Ascensión, a priest whose mission was in California just after the turn of the seventeenth century. Like many of his brothers, he addresses both the spiritual and temporal interests of the crown:

. . . the Spaniards in this place will be able to establish fisheries for pearls and other fish, of which there is an abundance, to send to New Spain, to sell in Mexico. Very good salt works can be established; likewise they can work mines of which there are some nearby. . . . These things being settled with the peace, love, and good will of the natives, the religious will give their attention to the ministry, and make a beginning and commencement of converting the Indians, in the way which may seem best to them, founding with great prudence and gentleness the new Christian Church to be planted there.

Granted full approval of the viceroy, Fray Agustín Rodríguez joined forces with Francisco Sánchez Chamuscado, Hernán Gallegos, and Pedro de Bustamante. He enlisted two other Franciscans, Fray Francisco López and Fray Juan de Santa María, to accompany him and assist in converting the members of various tribes. Riding behind nine armed men and their servants, the padres headed northward.

Once the party had moved beyond the stronghold of Spanish authority, its disposition began to shift radically. The Franciscans' avowed purpose was to carry the gospel to the Indians; indeed, that was the only reason the viceroy would license the expedition and permit it to leave Mexico. But Chamuscado and his companions, typical of most Spaniards in the New World, were primarily interested in discovering gold and silver and, failing that, in at least locating potential mining sites. The group was soon divided over their separate interests and, predictably, serious problems arose.

A few months into the expedition, Juan de Santa María secretly broke away from Chamuscado and the others. His purpose was twofold. He intended to report the soldiers' insubordinate behavior to the authorities in Mexico and to recruit additional priests to minister to the pueblos. However, his mission ended tragically. Indians apparently found him asleep on the trail and killed him with a large stone, a punishment they reserved for witches and others thought to be possessed by evil spirits.

Fray Santa María's death and its ominous implications notwithstanding, the party continued its explorations until midwinter. Then, when the expedition finally turned

ROADSIDE SHRINE, CHIMAYO

back toward Mexico, the two remaining priests separated themselves from Chamuscado's party and elected to stay and continue their work with the Indians.

Chamuscado died during the return journey. Gallegos, acting as spokesman, related the party's reluctance to leave the two priests behind, then in almost the same breath he delivered a glowing report of the quiescent riches to be found in New Mexico. Once again the fecund Spanish imagination was set into motion, the dream rekindled, the memory of previous failures elided.

The two priests who had remained in one of the native villages generated great concern among their Franciscan brothers. From the convent in Durango, Fray Bernardo Beltrán spoke out, proposing to take help to Fray Agustín Rodríguez and Fray Francisco López. With that end in mind he began to put together an expedition. Antonio de Espejo—a man of wealth originally from Córdoba who had fled to the upper reaches of Mexico after being indicted as an accomplice in a murder charge, a detail possibly unknown to the Franciscan community—got wind of the planned expedition and offered to underwrite the trip and accompany Fray Beltrán, ostensibly to protect him. As he wrote in his own "Report": "I made an offer in the belief that by so doing I was serving Our Lord and His Majesty—to accompany the friar and spend a portion of my wealth in defraying his costs and in supplying a few soldiers both for his protection and for that of the friars he meant to succor and bring back."

Gallegos's stories of riches would certainly have reached Espejo, as such news circulated rapidly throughout the sparsely populated outposts of the mining frontier. No one yet had been legally allowed to explore the territory north of Mexico; it was always mandatory to have the blessing of the crown. At least two renegades had made attempts at conquest; both had been reprimanded or brought to judgment. However, as Espejo would have known, an expedition under the guise of a religious mission was an entirely different matter.

The small group was assembled and provisioned, but for Fray Beltrán it got off to an unfortunate start. A second priest who had been scheduled to accompany him failed to turn up in time. Fray Beltrán was left the only priest on the expedition and, as time would show, though he had organized the company, he became relatively powerless against the wishes of Espejo and his soldiers.

CRUCIFIX, ESPANOLA

At Puaray the Spaniards discovered a wall painting, hastily covered over by the people of the village, that celebrated the deaths of Agustín Rodríguez and Francisco López. With that discovery, the priest's question was answered and the real purpose of their mission satisfied. But Espejo had other ideas. He was eager to see more of the pueblos, more of the country. His real purpose was to know where the gold and silver could be found. In fact, he hoped to bring back evidence of such overwhelming economic promise that the king would name him to lead the long-pending mission to colonize New Mexico, a prize eagerly sought by many wealthy Spaniards in Mexico.

Espejo ranged wide, combing the land for evidence of gold or silver. He led his small band of soldiers to the home of the Zunis and westward to the Hopi mesas. Along the way, he took as captives two Indians. One managed to escape; the other he took back to Mexico, where he had him educated, hoping optimistically to use him as a translator when he returned to New Mexico at the head of the pacification and colonization party.

Espejo was tireless in his efforts to reenter New Mexico. To the viceroy and the king he wrote of his fervid desire to continue his explorations. "I beg your Majesty to please be assured of my zeal, so dedicated to the service of your Majesty, and consider it well that I should finish my life in the continuation of these discoveries and settlements; for with the estate, prominence, and friends that I possess, I promise to serve your Majesty with greater advantage than any others who are attempting to make a contract with you regarding this enterprise." Not surprisingly, Espejo failed to secure the king's bid, as he lacked both the money and the necessary political clout.

The Indian Espejo had trained, Pedro Oroz (who had taken the name of his teacher in Mexico), died before the colonizing expedition was realized; but Juan de Dios, one of the Indians Oroz had tutored, did travel north with the first colonists, serving as interpreter and scribe.

In the closing years of the sixteenth century, the Spanish crown finally acted upon its plan to settle New Mexico. Following years of negotiations and heated political argument, which continued right up to the final moment, Don Juan de Oñate was granted the authority to lead the colonizing expedition. He massed over four hundred men and their servants, a small contingent of churchmen, thousands of livestock, and hundreds of wagons and carts, and readied them at a staging site near Santa Barbara in northern Mexico.

On January 26, 1598, the expedition creaked into motion. More than six months later, on August 11, bringing to an end hundreds of miles of arduous travel over mountains and deserts and through the rugged foothill country along the Rio Grande, Oñate and his escort of soldiers, riding out far in advance of the main party, chose a Tewa pueblo as the site for their headquarters. This pueblo, which the Tewa people called Ohke, was one of the villages Captain Barrionuevo had visited almost sixty years earlier.

Conducting himself in the manner of Coronado, with great enthusiasm but little regard for the Indians or their property, Oñate drove the Tewa people out of their pueblo. He annexed its storehouses and appropriated its rooms and dwellings for his own people. Then he renamed it San Juan de los Caballeros.

On August 18 the main group of colonists, soldiers, and adventurers, in a caravan that stretched out for miles along the trail, began arriving at the pueblo. A cross was planted and blessed at San Juan. Before a week had passed, Oñate's people had begun building a church large enough to accommodate their number. It was completed September 7 and blessed the following day. For the Spaniards, that deed signaled the start of civilization in New Mexico.

DEATHHEAD PALMA,
LOS MATACHINES DE ALCALDE

The Delicate Magic of Life

*In the dust where we have buried the silent races and
their abominations we have buried so much of the
delicate magic of life.*

D. H. LAWRENCE

For almost five centuries, people full of high purpose have gravitated toward the Southwest. The Franciscans came first, accompanying the soldiers and treasure seekers with Oñate; they vowed to transform the natives, to salvage their souls and further glorify the crown. Some years later, a handful of artists sought out New Mexico, especially the northern part of the state, as a place of inspiration and work. Gold fever had long since died out—once people accepted the reality that little treasure of significance was to be found.

The new adventurers, the writers, painters, photographers, and other artists who came in the nineteenth and twentieth centuries, were drawn by the land. Its geography of simple, elegant forms was configured by what many maintained was an underlying magic. The artists—Frank Hamilton Cushing, Adolph Bandelier, Charles F. Lummis, Peter Moran, Edward Curtis, Willard L. Metcalf, Gerald Cassidy, and Ernest L. Blumenschien, among others—were fascinated by the people of the two dominant cultures: the Pueblo people, whose culture some felt represented an exemplary form of life, and the Hispanic people, whose culture was in many ways just as mysterious as the Native

American culture and no more accessible. Unlike the Franciscans and other missionaries, who came originally to transform the natives, the new arrivals, at least in part, came to learn from them.

Typical of many of these latter-day travelers and possibly the most willful of them all was Mabel Dodge. She arrived in the Southwest after assuming a position of prominence among the cultural elite of Europe and New York. In some ways Mabel epitomized an affluent part of American culture at the turn of the century. She wanted to be associated with avant-garde art and thought, and to that end she used her money to gain access to the minds of the best artists and thinkers. She was ambitious and enthusiastic, and like a magnet she drew to her an astonishing array of people.

Mabel was something of a misfit. Always eager to find a niche for herself, it appears that no matter how hard she tried she never quite felt comfortable anywhere. Born in 1879 into a well-to-do Buffalo, New York, family and brought up conservatively, she longed to break with those conventions and be a new woman. In July 1900 she married Karl Evans, who two years later fathered her only child, John. Karl Evans died in a hunting accident in 1903 and Mabel, who had developed a strong interest in poetry, art, and ideas, traveled to Paris. There she met the architect Edwin Dodge, and they were married in October of 1904. Together they moved to Florence and created an incredible house, the Villa Curonia. Here Mabel established her first salon, attracting such luminaries as Eleanora Duse, Bernard Berenson, and Leo and Gertrude Stein.

After eight years at the Villa Curonia—years of desperate mood swings, her marriage veering toward disaster—Mabel left Florence and returned to the United States, eventually settling in Greenwich Village. While Edwin maintained a separate residence, she again established a salon, seeking out the company of the best minds in the arts, politics, and the social sciences. "That I was leading an existence without any real direction occurred to me over and over again," Mabel wrote in *Movers and Shakers*. "I had been caught in the whirlpool of contemporary agitation and I seemed to be going helplessly around in circles, though perhaps my reserved expression made onlookers believe I was a leading influence who knew what she was about.

"The fact is, I had rapidly become a mythological figure right in my own lifetime which, I am sure, is a rather rare experience. But the faculty I had for not saying much and yet for being there gave people's imaginations a chance to fabricate their own Mabel Dodge, which they did, attributing to her all kinds of faculties and powers."

She held the pose long enough to become a recognized power broker of new twentieth-century thinking. She hosted gatherings of people of enormous influence: Lincoln Steffens, Margaret Sanger, Edwin Arlington Robinson, A. A. Brill, Amy Lowell, Alfred Stieglitz, Carl Van Vechten, and even the young Walter Lippmann, among others. She had avant-garde culture at her fingertips. John Reed, the leftist writer, frequented the salon and became Mabel's friend, then her lover.

Edwin Dodge divorced Mabel in 1916. Having by then broken with Reed, Mabel went on to marry her third husband, the artist Maurice Sterne, in 1917. It was Sterne who led her to the Southwest. Seeking subject matter for his paintings, he had traveled alone to Santa Fe that year. After attending an Indian dance, he was convinced that he had found something that would attract and perhaps transform Mabel. He wrote begging her to join him. "Do you want an object in life?" he asked in one letter. "Save the Indians, their art — culture — reveal it to the world!"

Mabel arrived in Santa Fe a few weeks later. She tested the town, deemed it too cloying and civilized in a way she disliked, and moved seventy miles north to Taos. It was to be the most important move of her life.

As Maurice had predicted, Mabel was captivated by New Mexico. She was awed by the beauty of the land, the quaint otherworldliness of the people, and the open clarity of the air and sky. In *Edge of Taos Desert* she recalls her first morning in Santa Fe: "Maurice's house shone in the deep yellow sunshine which flooded the three little rooms and made one ashamed of ill humor. From the very first day I found that the sunshine in New Mexico could do almost anything with one: make one well if one felt ill, or change a dark mood and lighten it. It entered one's deepest places and melted the thick slow densities. It made one feel good. That is, alive."

Mabel recognized her new calling. Her salon, once a forum for fresh and radical ideas, she now dedicated to the Indian. It became her mission, a calling of greater magnitude than a socialite's whimsical crusade for a worthy cause.

FOUR GENERATIONS OF PUEBLO POTTERS

YOUNG PUEBLO DANCER

Within a short time of her arrival in Taos, she met Tony Luhan. In this extraordinary Taos Pueblo man she felt she had discovered an essence that gave her the courage to begin life again and this time to experience it fully, with real feeling.

> To start all over, to start living at last, to give up all the old ways, the old adapted ways of enduring this existence without being truly a part of it. . . . There followed two other realizations that were also momentous and radical, and were obviously the consequence of birth and feeling. One was that I was his forever and he was mine, and the other was that I could leave the world I had been so false in, where I had always been trying to play a part and always feeling unrelated, a world that was on a decline so rapid one could see people one knew dropping to pieces day by day, a dying world with no one appearing who would save it, a decadent world, where the bright, hot, rainbow flashes of corruption were the only light high spots. Oh, I thought, to leave it, to leave it all, the whole world of it and not be alone. To be with someone real at last, alive at last, unendingly true and untarnished.

Mabel was audacious; but after so many years she was ready to submit. She loved the land of New Mexico for what it was—honest and uncompromising. It overwhelmed her just as Tony did. To her credit, she thought of the land and Indians as one and the same thing; and her enthusiasm and efforts aided them in their fight to retain their land. Although she married Tony Luhan, from her writings one senses that she never fully understood the Indians; even as she reached out to embrace the life she saw in Tony and his culture, that raw tribalness to which D. H. Lawrence alluded, she seems again to have lost her way. In time, however, her passionate search produced in her a new eloquence and she stepped out of her role as patron and hostess to become an artist.

Characteristically, Mabel set about persuading her wide circle of friends from the East to join her efforts to preserve the Indian way of life. She intimated that in the process they might also be saving themselves, as she thought she was doing, by discovering in Indian culture what she interpreted as the pure integrity of tribal roots. Among those who responded, finally, was John Collier, who had known Mabel in New York before 1920.

Mary Austin, one of Mabel's earliest visitors in Taos, stopped in New Mexico on her way to Mexico. She had frequented Mabel's salon in Greenwich Village during her own stint there. She later recalled the experience in her autobiography: "Mabel I had met in New York, where she maintained a sort of radical salon where I had been entertained." Prior to their meeting, Mary Austin had published a series of Paiute Indian legends, written the introductory essay to *The Path of the Rainbow*, a collection of Indian songs, and utilized her Indian research in writing a play entitled *The Arrow Maker*. Drawing on her knowledge of Indian lore, she had lectured to Mabel's New York group, possibly even affording Mabel her first real look at the American Indian.

Like Mabel, Mary Austin loved the Southwest. Her descriptions of the landscape, while as romantic as Mabel's, are more succinct. "By land," she wrote, "I mean all those things common to a given region: the flow of the prevailing winds, the succession of veg-etal cover, the legend of ancient life; and the scene, above everything the magnificently shaped and colored scene." Perhaps her different view of the reality of New Mexico and the Indians was the result of necessity. Unlike Mabel, Mary Austin was forced to sup-port herself, along with her retarded child and an invalid husband. In New Mexico she took a job with the Carnegie Foundation, studying conditions in the pueblos in the northern part of the state.

Although Mary maintained a lasting friendship with Mabel Dodge, it was an uneasy and competitive bond. The two had similarly flamboyant styles and shared an interest in certain mystic pursuits in their reading and thinking that might have made access to the world of the Native Americans appear to be a natural step. Whatever their similar inter-ests, Mary knew her limits with Mabel. When she returned to New Mexico in 1924, she took up residence in Santa Fe, wisely avoiding a strain on their relationship, which very likely survived simply because of the distance between their two towns.

It has been said that Willa Cather was also one of Mabel's artists. The fact is that Cather traveled to the Southwest six years before Mabel arrived. During her initial trip, made in 1911, she gathered material that was included in *The Professor's House*. The section called "Tom Outland's Story"—often collected as a separate novella—is set in New Mexico, adding a sense of light and color to the novel's otherwise somber mid-western setting.

Not until 1925 did Cather return to New Mexico; then she came to embark on her novel *Death Comes for the Archbishop.* She stayed with Mary Austin in Santa Fe during the weeks she spent interviewing people and conducting background research into the land and history of New Mexico. Mabel invited her to Taos. There Cather met Tony Luhan, who showed her Taos Pueblo and the surrounding country; her encounter with him probably provided the inspiration for the character of Eusabio.

It is clear from Cather's writing that like Mabel Dodge Luhan and Mary Austin she was moved by a power she found in the landscape, and that, in turn, added eloquence to her work: "The sandy soil of the plain had a light sprinkling of junipers, and was splotched with masses of blooming rabbit brush, —that olive-coloured plant that grows in high waves like a tossing sea, at this season covered with a thatch of bloom, yellow as gorse, or orange like marigolds." And she often used the land symbolically, as in her description of the Sangre de Cristo Mountains: "Yes, Sangre de Cristos; but no matter how scarlet the sunset, those red hills never became vermilion, but a more and more intense rose-carnelian; not the colour of living blood, the Bishop had often reflected, but the colour of the dried blood of saints and martyrs preserved in old churches in Rome, which liquifies upon occasion."

Though they were not close, Mabel and Cather were comfortable with each other. Mabel attempted to interest Cather in the work she was doing on behalf of the Indian; but Cather, ever wary of compromising her talent, backed away from the idea gracefully, preferring, it seems, to let her eloquent fiction serve as her contribution.

Mabel's biggest literary coup was to convince D. H. Lawrence and his wife, Frieda, to visit New Mexico. Lawrence came, but he did so with reluctance and he hardly expected to be pleased, a sentiment he expressed in a letter to his friend S. S. Koteliansky: "Mabel Sterne, who is a rich American woman, lends us this new and very charming *adobe* house which she built for us: because she wants me to *write* this country up. God knows if I shall. America is more or less as I expected: shove or be shoved. But it has a bigness, a sense of space, and a certain sense of rough freedom, which I like."

Lawrence had only just arrived when Mabel dispatched him on a trip to an Apache ceremonial dance. He based his first essay about the country upon that experience. "And here, I am," he wrote, "a lone lorn Englishman, tumbled out of the world of the British Empire on to this stage: for it persists in seeming like a stage to me, and not like the proper world."

To Frieda's sister he observed: "Everything in America goes by *will*. A great negative *will* seems to be turned against all spontaneous life—there seems to be no *feeling* at all—no genuine bowels of compassion and sympathy: all this gripped, iron, *benevolent* will which in the end is diabolic. How can one write about it, except analytically?"

Mabel must have been distressed by Lawrence's initial reactions. His views of the culture and his desire to remain separate from it were radically different from hers, as can be seen from his conclusion to "Indians and an Englishman":

> I don't want to live again the tribal mysteries my blood has lived long since. I don't want to know as I have known, in the tribal exclusiveness. But every drop of me trembles still alive to the old sound, every thread in my body quivers to the frenzy of the old mystery. I know my derivation. I was born of no virgin, of no Holy Ghost. Ah, no these old men telling the tribal tale were my fathers. I have a dark-faced bronze-voiced father far back in the resinous ages. My mother was no virgin. She lay in her hour with this dusky-lipped tribe father. And I have not forgotten him. But he, like many an old father with a changeling son, he would like to deny me. But I stand on the far edge of their firelight, and am neither denied nor accepted. My way is my own, old red father; I can't cluster at the drum any more.

At the onset, Lawrence appears to have been overwhelmed by the stark New Mexican landscape. He was also guarded about moving too rapidly into the complexities of

Native American culture—though he may merely have been reacting against Mabel's enthusiasm. He found fault; he fought the country, pointing up its shortcomings. But much later, after he had bonded to the land, responding more with its vastness, its visual and spiritual rhythms, his attitude shifted dramatically.

> New Mexico, one of the United States, part of the U.S.A. New Mexico, the picturesque reservation and playground of the eastern states, very romantic, old Spanish, red Indian, desert mesas, pueblos, cowboys, penitentes, all that old film stuff. Very nice, the great Southwest, put on a sombrero and knot a red kerchief round your neck, to go out to the great free spaces!
>
> That is the New Mexico wrapped in absolutely hygienic and shiny mucous-paper of our trite civilization. That is the New Mexico known to most of the Americans who know it at all. But break through the shiny sterilized wrapping, and actually touch the country, and you will never be the same again.

Lawrence had ripped off the "mucous-paper" and the country had touched him, as Mabel had hoped it would.

"I think New Mexico was the greatest experience from the outside world that I have ever had," he continued in his essay for *Graphic Survey*. "It certainly changed me forever. Curious as it may sound, it was New Mexico that liberated me from the present era of civilization, the great era of material and mechanical development.

"The moment I saw the brilliant, proud morning shine over the deserts of Santa Fe, something stood still in my soul."

Except for a few of the more adventuresome souls, the artists associated with northern New Mexico spent only brief, though significant, periods in the Espanola Valley. They used the land and then moved on. Paul Strand was a visitor. For three summers, he rented a house in Taos from Mabel Dodge Luhan and went out to photograph the adobe architecture and the indigenous people. The California photographer Adam Clark Vroman shot the pueblos along the Rio Grande. Ansel Adams photographed his celebrated *Moonrise over Hernandez* (taken in midafternoon and not at night, as it appears in the manipulated print) from a point just above the little village of Hernandez, north of Espanola. John Marin, John Sloan, Stuart Davis, Marsden Hartley, and other painters from the East wandered the local hills in search of subject matter.

Only Georgia O'Keeffe came to spend any length of time in the Espanola Valley. She knew it and loved it. The local landscape inspired such works as the strange and moody painting of the black cross at Alcalde, where she lived for a winter. In the end, however, she chose to keep her distance. She worked at Ghost Ranch or in her low adobe perched at the edge of Abiquiu, with the valley in view. Of this she wrote: "Two walls of my room in the Abiquiu house are glass and from one window I see the road toward Espanola."

Land and sky met in O'Keeffe's paintings, and she used these spare elements like an alchemist working with base metals or a mystic with words.

THE APPROACH TO ESPANOLA

Coming to the Land

That land is a community is the basic concept of ecology, but that land is to be loved and respected is an extension of ethics. That land yields cultural harvest is a fact long known, but latterly often forgotten.

ALDO LEOPOLD

My curiosity about D. H. Lawrence first drew me to New Mexico. His ashes brought me here when I was eighteen, just as a year later his writings so intrigued me that I was compelled to visit Mexico.

New Mexico then was raw and more foreign than it is today. Its remote location, obscure history, and cultural difference prompted people to travel to it with the same caution they exercised when visiting a strange country. From Albuquerque I followed the old highway that twisted along the Rio Grande to Taos. I ate lunch on the Taos plaza, thumbing my copy of *Studies in Classic American Literature,* and then continued northward to Lawrence's burial place at San Cristobal.

The shrine at the ranch, decorated by Dorothy Brett, was so garish that it made me uncomfortable. I backed outside as soon as I had seen it, walked away, and stood looking down over the vast land that swept suddenly south to the Rio Grande Gorge. I preferred to associate that starkly beautiful image with Lawrence's memory. Finally, no longer inclined to remain near the shrine, I returned to my car and drove back to Albuquerque.

In 1977, when I mentioned the incident to Dorothy Brett, the painter who had been a friend of both Lawrence and Mabel, I said simply that I associated Lawrence more with the "great free spaces" he had written about than the cloying walls of the shrine. As she paused to consider my words, she drew her silver trumpet away from her ear and fingered the huge clunky silver cross that hung from her neck. I feared I had offended her. But at last she cooed: "Oh, Lorenzo would have liked that!"

Finally it was the land that brought me back. I had studied its history as if it were a part of my own life; I had come to find a place in it, to share its magic.

Autumn was at its peak. The cottonwoods had taken on the hues of polished gold and there was the slight smokiness of Indian summer still on the air. Though I did not remember the little town of Alcalde, which lies less than two miles from San Juan de los Caballeros, I had never forgotten that pueblo and my drive along the Rio Grande to Lawrence's ranch.

The place my wife and I found to buy in Alcalde was not a simple dwelling but more like a chronicle of small-town life. Offered with the living quarters were a bar, general store, and filling station. The building, actually a number of buildings collected under a single roof, had also served as dancehall, poolhall, and bootlegger's distillery, functions that had long passed out of use.

The town was unlike any we had seen. We might have entered a time warp, withdrawing to another world where life ran at a far slower pace. Along the unpaved main street an old man in a broad-brimmed hat herded a band of bleating ewes; he took the sheep around the adobe church, crowded them into a narrow lane, and drove them out of sight. The *ristras* of red chile hung from outside vigas were a part of the people's everyday diet, to be ground and used.

The sons and daughters of the old woman who owned the house and ran the store were congregating for Thanksgiving. Two of the men, standing in the yard, backs to us, stopped their conversation and focused their attention away, on the mountains to the east. The women were in the kitchen, preparing food for the next day. The smells that drifted out to the rest of the house were seductive—of chile, onions, garlic, *posole*, the great natural scents of New Mexican cuisine.

Here in the north, concern for the old people continued to mold the lives of their children. The pattern reached back centuries. These sons and daughters were considering selling the house because their mother was no longer able to take care of her businesses; she had been robbed and abused. Her children feared for her safety. There were sentimental considerations. This was the inheritance they would share. They had been born in these rambling rooms, their lives shaped here. There were misgivings about selling. But they were trying to be practical.

Under those conditions, a careful examination of the house was difficult. One of the sons, a teacher, showed us around. He had moved home after a divorce, and now he wanted to simplify his life by closing down the store and bar and moving his mother and himself into a new double-wide trailer with wood paneling and wall-to-wall carpeting. He rubbed his hands together and cleared his throat nervously as he hurried us from room to room.

The store was a long and badly lighted room whose shelves were sparsely stocked with tinned food, candles, bread, candy, and such essentials as flour, cooking oil, and matches. A tall, upright cash register stood on the counter. In the back sat a cooler for soft drinks and ice cream. An antique Wurlitzer, flanked by small tables and fraying Mexican chairs, dominated the bar. An oval-framed portrait of a father or grandfather, neck stiffened by a high collar, full mustache obscuring his lips, hung from a high nail over an archway. Farther into the house stood a rack of clothes that reeked of mothballs and dust. The room next to the dancehall was stacked to the ceiling with boxes of apples, their sweet, winey smell heavy in the air.

In the end, I was most impressed by the spacious rooms. Space had been what we wanted and had failed to find—in Santa Fe, and in the tiny, low-ceilinged adobe rooms of the dozens of houses we had seen scattered throughout three counties of New Mexico. Space was something we yearned for, indeed something we really *needed* after a decade of life in New York City.

Sometime in the past, the old buildings had been plastered. That ancient yellow coat, sanded down by wind and grit, had aged and begun to crumble, exposing bits of chicken wire and the dull gray undercoat. But beneath its patchy surface, we'd been assured, was adobe, the first block of which had been laid in the last century. Adobe was an important element to us. Adobe tied the place to its past. It reinforced the mystery.

The village, with its odd pockets of growth and deterioration, reminded me of small towns in Sonora or the desolate country beyond Ensenada in Baja California. There were walls, but they were unlike the fortress-high enclosures of colonial Mexico. Some had collapsed into ruined heaps. There were traditional family compounds, but many were coming apart, old ties beginning to fray. Mobile homes destroyed their continuity. Some places had drifted into decline. Back in shoulder-high pigweed and lamb's-quarter lay the carcasses of cast-off refrigerators, washing machines, and kitchen stoves. Whole yards had been dedicated to preserving the wasted remains of a family's entire investment in the automobile.

The dirt road running south made a jog to the west and then turned abruptly south again, where it met the irrigation ditch, the lifeline of the community. From there to Swan Lake Ranch it was lined with cottonwoods. Branches arched low over the road, and where the yellow leaves caught the late afternoon sun they blazed with a golden, glowing light. A mile farther and we wound up from the river bottom and climbed to San Juan Pueblo.

The Tewa had called this pueblo Ohke. Don Juan de Oñate, the Spanish conquistador, had chosen it for his headquarters and created the first territorial capital, the first settlement in the Southwest, one that predated both Jamestown and Plymouth. In his calculating letters back to the viceroy and the king, he describes his findings here with eloquence and no little exaggeration:

> It is a land abounding in flesh of buffalo, goats with hideous horns, and turkeys; and in Mohoce there is game of all kinds. There are many wild and ferocious beasts, lions, bears, wolves, tigers, *penicas*, ferrets, porcupines, and other animals, whose hides they tan and use. Toward the west there are bees and very white honey, of which I am sending a sample. Besides, there are vegetables, a great abundance of the best and greatest salines in the world, and many kinds of very rich ores.

STOREKEEPER AND CHILD, ALCALDE

We rounded the turn and drove into San Juan Pueblo, which had been inhabited by the Tewa since about A.D. 1300. Like most of the valley, the pueblo gives up its history reluctantly, in bits and pieces. The Indians at San Juan acknowledge that their forebears moved from a higher terrain to the river not because of a dwindling moisture base—as many major archaeological theories maintain—but because of pestilence and epidemic.

The San Juan people's journey is clearly depicted in mythic history. According to legend, the Tewa originally lived somewhere north of their present homes, in Sipofene under Sandy Place Lake. The world there was entirely dark; men and animals lived together and knew no death. They wanted a way out of this dark world so they dispatched a man to explore the other world. He met the animals and learned how to survive. His people rejoiced. Stars and the rainbow were named. There was hope. Seeing that, the people ventured forth—cautiously. They met with sickness; they discovered evil. Government was created and leaders appointed to oversee various aspects of life. The world was becoming more complex, the life of the people more fragile. Death was created, and life became more like we know it today. Gradually the people were forced to move south, the migration that eventually brought the Tewa to their present pueblo.

Some of the older adobes, still in use though now modernized, dated back to those times. Others had begun to deteriorate. The ribs of a caved-in roof strained light onto a dirt floor. A few buildings had simply crumbled and been absorbed back into the earth. To the south and east stood the new government housing, tiny shoebox structures laid out on a grid, like the suburbs that had sprung up all across America after World War II. Architecturally, their only conspicuous tie to the old pueblo was an occasional *horno,* the domed outdoor oven introduced by the Spaniards, many of which were already smoking or being readied for a Thanksgiving feast the next day.

From the crumbling fragments still evident at San Juan, one can begin to formulate a local history. Remnants of the old pueblo form its core and tie the present settlement back to the ancient civilizations of the Southwest. Tribal members maintain that San Juan's modern appearance, with a state highway forking through it in two directions, is deceptive; the pueblo's traditions, they insist, are sound. Perhaps to reinforce that theory, the San Juan gaming establishment, Okhay Casino—housing Indian bingo, video slots, and poker—was constructed along the highway, well away from the old pueblo.

The houses on the original plaza were created to correspond with the landscape that encompasses the pueblo. The layout is part of the overall ritual of life that reminds the Tewa people of their orientation to the cosmos. Distant mountains mark the cardinal directions and also set the north-south and east-west axes of the pueblo. The closer flat-top hills serve like great protective altars. The ancient pattern, configured by sacred lakes and shrines, is as old as ritual life itself.

Whereas Anglos are often at odds with the land, Native Americans have always harmonized their lives with its rhythms. To the native people, these low buildings house a pantheon of Pueblo gods. Each home has been built with a blessing; each has a life of its own, a purpose beyond its function as a dwelling.

Two churches stood on either side of the highway, both Catholic. The older was of quarried stone, constructed in the French style, a carryover from the reign of Bishop Jean-Baptiste Lamy and the European priests he brought in to support an autocratic regime that ran painfully counter to the Hispanic and Native American cultures; it looked oddly like a building one might see in France, where quarried stone was a far more familiar commodity. The newer church stood across the road to the west. It was built of brick in a singularly colorless American Gothic design that held up badly when compared to some of the great local churches such as the mother church at Santa Cruz, El Santuario in Chimayo, or San Jose in Las Trampas.

In 1625, during his four-year appraisal of the missions of New Mexico, Fray Alonzo de Benavides visited San Juan. "In relation to the church," he wrote in flowing long-hand, "the buildings of the pueblo are to the north. Three tenements, separated from one another at the corners, and the Epistle side of the church enclose a plaza of ordinary size. In addition, opposite the church and about a pistol shot from that facade are two small tenements that make a kind of street, for one is back of the other and both face south."

Tacked around the edges of the old pueblo, which remained much the same as Benavides had seen it, were schools, the tribal police station and courtroom, a general store, the post office, and shops selling local arts and crafts. Most of the new buildings had the appearance of an army outpost, though they'd been constructed in imitation of Pueblo style and coated with adobe-colored stucco. But at the heart of the pueblo, the low buildings clinging together to frame the dirt plazas, which tremble slightly under the pounding steps of each ceremonial dance, glowed with a patina left by centuries of use.

As architecture, the buildings mimicked the surrounding mesas and the strata of the natural landscape. They'd been built out of dirt, adobe mixed from sand and clay and bonded with straw to create material at once fragile and strong. Their builders possessed a natural genius for harmonious design, a quality lost upon the Spaniards, who found little to admire in the Indians' ideas. But a few of the travelers who came later did recognize the significance of their abilities as builders and farmers.

In 1831 Josiah Gregg, then working as a trader in Santa Fe, began a series of notes on what he observed during his travels, and thirteen years later they were published as *Commerce of the Prairies*, a book that remains a classic of its kind. He devoted one chapter to the "Wild Indians," echoing a view held by many people about the tribes of the Rio Grande, and another chapter to the pueblos:

> Although the term *Pueblo* in Spanish literally means the people, and their *towns*, it is here specifically applied to the *Christianized Indians* (as well as their villages)—to those aborigines whom the Spaniards not only subjected to their laws, but to an acknowledgment of the Romish faith, and upon whom they forced baptism and the cross in exchange for the vast possessions of which they had robbed them. All that was left them was, to each Pueblo, a league or two of land situated around their villages, the conquerors reserving to themselves at least ninety nine hundredths of the whole domain as a requital for their generosity. When these regions were first discovered it appears that the inhabitants lived in comfortable houses and cultivated the soil, as they have continued to do up to the present time. Indeed, they are now considered the best horticulturalists in the country, furnishing most of the fruits and a large portion of the vegetable supplies that are to be found in the markets. They were until very lately

the only people in New Mexico who cultivated the grape. They also maintain at the present time considerable herds of cattle, horses, etc. They are, in short, a remarkably sober and very industrious race, conspicuous for morality and honesty, and very little given to quarrelling or dissipation, except when they have had much familiar intercourse with the Hispano-Mexican population.

Apparently, Oñate was never comfortable at San Juan. A few weeks after settling in the pueblo, he moved his entire camp to Yunque-yunque, a somewhat larger village across the Rio Grande; after displacing the Tewas once again, he renamed it San Gabriel and set about remodeling and building to fit his needs. There he remained until the capital was moved to Santa Fe in 1610.

We drove over the one-lane bridge to the spot where San Gabriel once stood. Only faint traces of the old walls could be seen. A severe, unadorned concrete cross had been erected on the hillside just north of the road, and near it was a plaque placed by the New Mexico State Society of Daughters of the American Colonists that read:

> JULY 11, 1598, JUAN DE OÑATE,
> COLONIZER, ESTABLISHED THE FIRST
> SPANISH CAPITAL IN THIS PUEBLO.
> THE INDIANS RECEIVED THE SPANIARDS
> WITH GREAT COURTESY. THEREAFTER
> THE PUEBLO WAS KNOWN AS SAN JUAN
> DE LOS CABALLEROS. LATER OÑATE
> MOVED THE CAPITAL INTO LARGER
> QUARTERS AND NAMED IT SAN GABRIEL.

Understandably, the Daughters of the American Colonists chose to believe that the Indians volunteered a "great courtesy" to their members' forebears; however, their claim is at odds with historic fact. The Indians were open with the Spaniards, yet their generosity was the product (at least in part) of naivete and fear. Such fear is evident from the journals of Gaspar Castano de Sosa in which he recorded his own trip into New Mexico in 1590–91: "When we arrived, no one came out to us, not even an Indian whom we had sent ahead from the previous pueblos. They showed great fear at seeing us, especially the women, who wept very much."

In fact, Gaspar Pérez de Villagra, who traveled with Oñate and chronicled the expedition, tells us in his *Historia* that the reference to caballeros is not to Oñate's men at all: "Not unlike shipwrecked mariners, after many trials and many sufferings, we came in sight of a splendid pueblo. We gave it the name of 'San Juan,' adding 'de los Caballeros' in memory of those noble sons who first raised in these barbarous regions the bloody tree upon which Christ perished for the redemption of mankind." "Noble sons" probably refers to the two priests who had been left behind by Fray Rodríguez and martyred in Puaray fifteen years earlier.

For all of Oñate's faults, his efforts should neither be discounted nor repudiated. In their own way, his accomplishments were monumental. He took enormous risks. He faced the difficult task of living in a hostile country, among natives about whom he knew little. He had made a sizable personal investment in the colonizing venture. He knew that Coronado before him had been ruined by his adventure, a fortune squandered, his reputation gone. Added to that worry, he was also disturbed by the impatience of the soldiers and colonists who had accompanied him. They had been in the country only a short time when the first threats of mutiny and desertion were voiced. The colonists, who had risked their lives and invested their own money, were clearly disappointed. This country was no equal to Mexico, as they had been led to believe by Oñate. Mexico, too, was often a fierce land, but its riches had proved abundant enough to offset the risks of conquest and make the hardships well worth enduring. Having seen nothing in New Mexico to whet their hopes, many wanted simply to cut their losses and leave.

In his attempt to hold them together, Oñate imposed a number of desperate and autocratic restrictions. For example, he strictly forbade the settlers to dispatch letters back to Mexico. In his own reports to his superiors, he exaggerated the importance of New Mexico and its potential for riches.

ALCALDE MAN

By 1601 Oñate could control the people no longer. He returned from an exploration of Quivira—another fruitless excursion to a location extolled for its wealth—to find that a group of his soldiers and colonists had fled back to Mexico.

In his second letter to the count of Monterrey, he wrote of the rebellion: "At the end of August I began to prepare the people of my camp for the severe winter which both the Indians and the nature of the land threatened me; and the devil, who has ever tried to make good his great loss occasioned by our coming, plotted, as is his wont, exciting a rebellion among more than forty-five soldiers and captains, who under the pretext of not finding immediately whole plates of silver lying on the ground, and offended because I would not permit them to maltreat these natives, either in their person or in their goods, became disgusted with the country, or to be more exact, with me, and endeavored to form a gang in order to flee to that New Spain."

There were, and there continue to be, those who champion Oñate's efforts. One Spaniard writing in his defense was Padre Jerónimo de Zárate Salmerón, a priest who built a church in the Jemez Pueblo and worked to convert the people there. In _Relaciones, An Account of Things Seen and Learned by Father Jerónimo de Zárate Salmerón_, the writer comes to Oñate's defense long after the governor had suffered the damaging testimony of the deserters and been banished from New Mexico and imprisoned in his own house while his trial dragged on. It is clear that Father Jerónimo knew of Oñate's appeal and final pardon before he undertook his book. He chose to romanticize the governor: "He established his camp between this river [the Rio Grande] and the Zama [Chama], partly because he wanted it there, and because some men with bad intentions have lied about it and defiled it, just for the sake of speaking evilly of the pueblo that Don Juan de Oñate founded, saying that it is bad and poor land. These are men who escaping have left fleeing, and when they are asked the cause of their departure, so as not to confess their crimes, tell these stories, defaming the land; and contradicting them I say this pueblo is very important and of very great moment and usefulness to this entire land, when and if the rest of it is settled."

Oñate continued his quest, driven by the dream of gold and great power. He, more than anyone else in the party, stood to benefit—or to lose—from whatever this raw country might serve up, and as he traveled throughout the Southwest his desperation increased. Doggedly, he followed up every lead, visiting each place, swallowing his disappointment, glossing over his findings in ebullient letters back to the viceroy.

Father Jerónimo had a curious perspective on Oñate; and his ideas about geography were equally eccentric. "Since the plan of D. Juan de Oñate was to form expeditions and to explore the land, he could not find a more convenient situation than this place, because of its being in the center of the realm, and because to the west of it California is 200 leagues away . . . and to the east, Florida is 300 leagues air distance, since we ought not to measure it by the distance that Orantes, Cabeza de Vaca, nor Hernando de Soto traveled, since they all wandered around lost, walking back and forth, and I am only calculating diametrically to the north."

Father Jerónimo's warped sense of geography was not radically different from my own as I stood at the concrete cross and attempted to calculate where I was in relationship to the few local landmarks I recognized. I continued up the spiny ridge above the site of San Gabriel, stepping over rocks and abundant prickly pear cactus, until I could look out across the tops of the massive cottonwoods that appeared to float above the *bosque* along the Rio Grande. I recalled the early assessment of this valley by the Swiss-born archeologist Adolph Bandelier. Nearly one hundred years before, almost to the day, in 1883, he had approached from the south and recorded the following: "The view from the 'puertecita' is a very striking one. The valley of Santa Cruz de la Cañada lies at the very feet, with the village and church. The Chimayo valley extends to the east of it. The Rio Grande bottom is plainly visible to the enormous canones and potreros on the west side, above which the high Sierra del Valle [Jemez Mountains] rise. These canones and potreros are very formidable. But the bottom of the valley itself is surprisingly fertile and beautiful. San Juan itself lies at the north end of the valley, almost opposite the confluence of the Rio Chama [and the Rio Grande]."

Little had changed. Above the river the land lay in parched orange and ocher hills, showing sparse vegetation. The Rio Grande, which cuts north to south through the entire length of New Mexico, was a glistening line of golden light. This great river, the single most important characteristic of the valley and perhaps of the entire state, is met to the south and west of San Juan Pueblo by the Chama River and farther south by the smaller Santa Cruz, which flows into it from the east. At this confluence, as in most places along the river's meandering course, the flood plain stretches to a maximum of only a few miles. Settlements cluster close to the rivers. They take their life from a narrow belt of alluvial land that is as vulnerable as it is fertile.

To the east lie the tallest mountains in New Mexico, the Sangre de Cristos, whose highest peaks, etched in afternoon light, tower to a point just above thirteen thousand feet. To the west are the Jemez Mountains, site of Valle Grande, reputedly the largest volcanic crater on the face of the earth.

During the period the Jemez volcano was active it spewed a thick layer of debris over an area at least fifty miles in radius. The aftermath of its massive eruptions brought drastic climatic changes to this section of the Southwest. The volcano's cooling magma created an increased humidity. This in turn produced rain and set into motion a concatenate cycle that would continue for an age. Plants, in order to renew themselves and survive, were forced to set roots and grow in the crust of volcanic debris. Gradually, as the tenacious flora of the high desert struggled back to life, the land mass surrounding the Espanola Valley must have looked very different from the rest of the Southwest— lusher, more fertile, with a subtropical climate.

An agricultural people settled near to its streams and rivers. These early inhabitants of the area left their story in fragments: tools, broken utensils, and whole villages of abandoned living quarters. We can judge the evolution of these people from such artifacts. Baskets daubed with mud gave way to simple, unadorned pots, and those were replaced by pottery bearing designs that reflect the observations and beliefs of its makers. The people moved from cave to pit house to multi-storied dwellings, a progression that has marked man's steady climb to civilization in almost every part of the world.

Terracing and other methods of advanced crop management, launched centuries before the Spaniards arrived, are apparent in sections of the country where today farming without irrigation is almost impossible and certainly impractical. We can surmise that the rains fell off gradually, the water table dropped, and the crops became less abundant. Inhabitants of pueblos such as Puye, Otowi, Tsankawi, and Sapawe, now mere ruins, were forced at some point to abandon their homes and move down toward the river, closer to the ever-shrinking sources of water. The pattern of their move may explain, for example, why the Indians finally abandoned the great settlements at Chaco Canyon one hundred miles to the west of the Jemez Mountains. This phenomenon is hardly unique to the Rio Grande. Throughout the arid regions of the world, the move to a river or any other source of water for survival is a part of the history of civilization; we see it along the Nile and other rivers of Africa as well as the Amazon and the receding rivers of South America.

On November 27, 1883, looking out over the Rio Grande, Bandelier observed: "This valley is charming, and as far as fertility is concerned, the handsomest I have seen in New Mexico."

Such was the world I had come to inhabit.

Looking north, beyond the vast *bosque* of golden cottonwoods, I knew that one of the clusters of houses close to the river would be Alcalde.

Already, I was thinking of it as home.

BUFFALO DANCERS

Enchanted Valley

Our original intention in starting for New Mexico had been to settle in Santa Fe. But all our plans were elastic ones, and we had taken with us an artistic compass whose needle, exquisitely sensitive to beauty, was liable to switch us off at any point on the route. It had already made our course a rather devious one, and I suppose that it only is to be held responsible for stranding us eventually in the out of the way little corner known as Espanola.

HARRISON
HARPER'S MAGAZINE
MAY 1885

From the cab of a thirty-four-foot rented truck, we found that most American cities and towns can be bypassed on the freeways. At first, we wanted to see them. But there was a sad monotony to the fraying of small main streets of the Southeast and South, too many businesses boarded up and shut down to make way for the malls, and we finally chose to stick to the outskirts. The open country was almost as forlorn. We encountered one after another the abandoned farm buildings on what were once homesteads that had been recently swallowed up by the agribusiness conglomerates listed on the stock exchange.

Then, as we drove into the Southwest, the country seemed to take on a new character.

TORITO, LOS MATACHINES DE ALCALDE

Rich infusions of color in the soil, a dramatic widening of the sky, and the clear air announced that we had finally put the Texas Panhandle between us and Oklahoma.

New Mexico is a unique, gentle land. Beyond Santa Fe, the pristine sun and sky are deceptively soft. Hills spotted with piñon give way to eroded mesas and snow-capped mountains. At night the air has the feel of chamois, and overhead the heavens are filled with stars. In time I would discover that it is also a deceptive country. Northern New Mexico can turn vicious and uncompromising, the beauty of the landscape becoming a thin veneer over a life as unpredictable as it is threatening.

In Alcalde I stopped in front of the place we had bought. It loomed larger than I remembered, its faults glaring. Dust, boiling up in the wake of the rented truck, rose in a cloud and slowly drifted away. For a long time I sat in the hot cab, tired, a little afraid to step inside the house. Finally, my body quivering from two thousand miles of highway, I climbed down from the truck to try the keys to the front door.

A seasoned adobe that has stood uninhabited for even a short time exudes the rich smells of earth and the outdoors. That smell greeted me when I unlocked the door and stepped inside the dark general store. The outlines of missing coolers and counters were mapped on the hardwood floor like a phantom history. My footsteps echoed as I surveyed improvements spanning almost a century—linoleum tile over hardwood floors, plywood paneling to mask the uneven adobe, a sagging checkerboard of acoustical ceiling tile tacked to the vigas, every square inch of which would need to be ripped out, dragged to the backyard, and burned.

One could sense the presence of the previous family. A neighbor who stopped by to introduce himself hinted that the spirit of the old man who'd been a bootlegger dwelt there yet. He claimed that even now the spirit of the old man stood guard over a copper still that he'd filled with money and buried somewhere beneath one of the floors. The man was itching to see if I would go for the fanciful story and start ripping up the boards.

People drove past, slowed their cars, had a good look at the rented truck, at us, and then crept on; a few moments later the same cars would return, idling slower, and stop, the occupants craning to watch as we carried the boxes inside.

A small group of young men perched on the low wall across the street studied our moves while they shared a bottle of MD 20/20. Two detached themselves from their friends and with their footsteps kicking up puffs of dry summer dust ventured across to where I was working.

The first one, whose name was Benny, announced that they—meaning their ancestors—had lived here for two hundred years.

"Three hundred, bro," corrected his companion, brow wrinkled with concern. *"Que no?"*

Yes. Three hundred years.

Actually, the Spaniards had settled San Juan—just two miles to the south—378 years before, a fact I might have mentioned but did not. Historical accuracy was not at issue. Benny had a point he wanted to make: I was a gringo and he felt I had no business moving into this community. He did not know how to say that in so many words, but it was what he meant. He retreated, along with his companion, back to their nearly empty bottle on the wall, his speech largely left unmade. In that confrontation I had been shown a side of the town I'd hoped to avoid.

One winter afternoon two years later, Benny staggered onto my porch during fiesta, picked a fight with a man from another town, and took a beating so serious that he left a twenty-foot trail of spattered blood in the snow along the driveway between my house and my neighbor's to the north.

It was difficult for the second youth—I'll call him José—to communicate at all. He was so numbed by the cheap wine that he fumbled the handshake. In the end, his friends were forced to shoulder his weight and lead him away.

Six weeks later, José showed up at the back door. He swayed on his feet and gesticulated with his right hand, holding his left hand guardedly against his stomach. When finally he thrust his left hand toward me, I took a step back, a wave of nausea washing over me. He had driven a two-tined fork from a carving set through his palm and then twisted it around upon itself.

He seemed almost as surprised at what he had done as I was. Blood dripped from his fingers, staining his pants and shoes. He kept trying to force his way into the house. I pushed him outside, pinned him against the wall, and attempted to talk to him. Nothing he said made sense. Finally, I led him across the road and my neighbor loaded him into his pickup and hauled him to the hospital emergency room in Espanola, where the fork was removed.

Over the next few years José served time for, among other things, rape charges involving a nun and an infant. One evening, less than a week after José had been released from prison, a van pulled up in front of his house. The guy in the passenger's seat shouted José's name, repeating it until José emerged onto the porch. When he appeared, squinting to see who had called to him, the side door of the van slid open and a hail of bullets cut him down where he stood. That night, in the hospital, he died.

Word on the street was that José got only what he deserved. I felt saddened by his fate, recognizing in it a familiar pattern confirmed by local history. One tragic aspect of life in northern New Mexico is the displaced and sadly wasted passions of many of its young men. In their veins still runs a trickle of blood from the conquistadors. Like their ancestors they hunger for recognition; they want to be noticed, to have something that will affirm their worth. But the world that might once have acknowledged that heritage has faded. So they hang out; they fight; they drink; they shoot up; they fall into useless routines. They run afoul of the law. They die in the streets. They crash and burn.

An increasing number of young people are venturing out to go to school or find work, but it is not in the tradition. Often the only opportunity the men from the valley have to alter their lives is to go away to war. Many have gained an awareness of the outside world and an introduction to the present century in the two world wars, in Korea, and in Vietnam.

Vietnam is a war that cannot be stopped. It produced among its casualties an army of addicts—stoned, disillusioned men now in their thirties and forties who roam the village streets and back roads of the Espanola Valley, looking for drugs and easy ways to pay for them. If ordinary boys from other parts of the country felt alienated after their discharge, the young men in this valley, who'd gone to Vietnam after the isolation of centuries, experienced a kind of double alienation.

Neighbors, Alcalde

MUSICIAN, ALCALDE

VINTAGE CHEVY, ALCALDE

During my first week in town, armed with knowledge about local history but ignorant to the workings of tradition, I called this condition culture shock. I was not mistaken. Culture shock had prevailed in the valley for almost four hundred years. There had been too many governments, too many new sets of laws imposed upon the people, too many flags. Most recently, the lab at Los Alamos, celebrating its fiftieth year in 1993, and representing yet another alien invasion, had drawn the valley people directly out of the eighteenth century and into the space age with dizzying speed.

Santa Fe would have been an easy move from New York or anyplace else. People make the transition to Santa Fe today the way they move to Aspen or La Jolla. They buy into the charm and dress the part, in cowboy hats and boots and bolo ties. But nobody takes up residence in the small towns of northern New Mexico without giving serious thought to the consequences.

I had heard unsettling stories about locals driving out gringos, robbing or burning their houses, with little or no sympathy from lawmen, and stories of rudeness and worse to the gringas. Nothing of the kind happened to us. We met the people up and down our road. They were mostly shy but genuine and quick to offer help. They volunteered information about the area. As crops ripened, many of our neighbors stopped their pickups in front of the house and dropped off sacks of corn, tomatoes, or chile. We were invited into homes at fiesta time to share traditional food and listen to stories of local customs.

Underlying every kind act, however, came a note of caution, which was understandable, though unsettling. For hundreds of years these northern pueblos, hamlets, and villages have existed as occupied territory, the people locked into their own closed cultures—speaking their own languages, attending to their own religions, often practicing their own medicine. The people were clearly suspicious of outsiders. Starting with the conquistadors, outsiders had always brought trouble and unwanted change.

The Indians clung to a history they felt bound to protect; they remained squarely in their culture. One sensed it at dances and from conversations with members of the tribes. They remembered their gods at the altars in their kivas and homes. Drums and the voices of singers resounded from the plazas on dance days, drawing the people together, each performance a celebration, a prayer of thanks, of supplication.

The local Hispanic people were not as backward as people sometimes characterized them—unkind treatment ironically reminiscent of the way their own Spanish ancestors had centuries earlier dismissed the Indians as savages and heathens. Local Hispanics modeled their lives on forebears whose existence had been threatened by time and forces beyond their control. They lived inside the boundaries of the United States, not by choice but because New Mexico had become a state. Many thought of themselves as Hispanics from northern New Mexico, foreigners in a gringo world. They recalled ancestors who had been informed of their rights and stripped of their land. Adjusting to the twentieth century had proved painful and confusing.

Some of the younger people who had been away to universities referred to themselves as Chicanos—because it had the ring of revolution. It tied them to a movement and gave them an identity. Many, embarrassed to be revolutionary, gravitated toward the Anglo culture. But it was a mere flirtation. "Some of us even started looking like you guys," one young man said to me. He did not smile.

At the other extreme were those who thought of themselves as _pura españoles_, pure Spanish. They visited Spain, going to the cities and villages from which, four hundred years ago or more, their forefathers had set out for the New World. One man described to me how he and his wife arrived in Spain, combed archives, found names, and introduced themselves to a few distant relatives. But there had been a gap of almost five hundred years between the last contact with these families, a period difficult to explain. In the end, the man and his wife had been disappointed and unnerved by the experience.

The local Hispanic heritage is a source of pride. But the difficult conditions of life in remote mountain towns and villages came with its own problems. The isolation unavoidably produced too many _primos_ and _tios_ and _tias_, too much inbreeding, too many damaged children, too many families living too close. Each had its consequences. Vicious feuds of long standing were common. Gun battles broke out between relatives and neighbors, the reasons behind them as diverse as the skirmishes over land and politics anywhere, internecine family battles provoked by money, birthright, or property. Nothing here was so different from what happens in much of the rest of the world, but the solutions here in the valley were often jarringly direct.

I am reminded of a skirmish that took place a few doors from my house, serious gunfire exchanged across a main street. Following an altercation one afternoon in which the name of the daughter of the first neighbor had been denigrated by the second, the parties opened fire with large-caliber deer rifles.

The battle began almost casually, with name calling and an initial exchange of shots. Lead slugs ripped into adobe walls and shattered glass. A second volley heated things up. And a third. By that time someone had phoned the state police. Sirens could be heard wailing all the way from Espanola. The black-and-white patrol cars barreled into town, emergency lights blazing, sirens piercingly close, and stopped short of the two houses. Using their cars as shields, the officers, seasoned to the hazards of law enforcement in northern New Mexico, where both feuding parties can turn on the police as the common enemy, addressed the two families through bullhorns. How the problem was resolved remains a mystery. An hour later, the cars from the state police and Rio Arriba Sheriff's Department reversed into the road and cleared out of town. No arrests had been made. The shooting had stopped. Life drifted back to normal.

LOWRIDERS, ESPANOLA

The Bare Threads
of Culture

. . . not only have the settlers of New Mexico not enjoyed riches, but the scourge of God has been on them always, and they are the most oppressed and enslaved people in the world for they are not the master of their wills nor estates, since with ease, and without their being able to put up any resistance, the riches are taken away from them by a strong hand, and they are left stark naked and people elsewhere are prosperous. These are secret judgments of God.

PILOT MORERA

We are a conquered people," Cathy Berryhill contends. "I hate to say it, but here in northern New Mexico we really are a conquered people. We always have been."

We sit in the late October sun outside the library at Northern New Mexico Community College, where Cathy teaches English. There is a breeze with a crisp edge, the first sign of an approaching cold front.

Though she grew up in Chimayo, Cathy has lost the strong accent characteristic of the Espanola Valley. She wears a dark long-sleeved dress and "sensible" shoes. Her glasses, with large lenses and ear pieces that swoop up from the bottom of the frames, and the way she keeps her hair pulled back in a tight bun, hint at a severity I do not find in her nature.

"We had no weapons," she says, describing New Mexico under occupation. "There were no malleable metals in New Mexico. We were never a metal society. Our lives have always revolved around dirt. Strictly dirt, the soil. All the metals that we ever got to make firearms or anything else out of, we had to either steal or bring in from somewhere else."

I point out that Spaniards have long been famous for their steel. Spanish swords, often reforged from horseshoes and bits of scrap by master craftsmen in Toledo and other cities, were prized for their superior design and durability.

"That's true," she concedes, "for Spain. But not us. We lost that art. The older people here still hoard metal—little hinges, old pieces of cars. They never throw away any metal because it used to be that the only metal to make anything out of was got by melting down the scrap you'd saved."

"This must explain the yards full of junk, the old cars and machinery I see in the valley."

"Absolutely. That kind of hoarding is in our genes." She pauses to call out to a male student emerging from the science building. "Hey, I was wondering about you! You passing everything? . . . That's great! I'm proud of you! Come and see me sometime."

She picks up the thread again. "When Kearny came over the Santa Fe trail, our people were standing on the bluff and could have ambushed a few of his soldiers, but the troops just kept coming. I mean by the thousands, regulars in uniforms with guns and cannons."

General Stephen W. Kearny led the United States Army of the West into New Mexico in 1846. His proclamation to New Mexico's governor, Manuel Armijo, addressed from Bent's Fort, contained a blunt pronouncement: "I come by orders of my government to take possession of the country over part of which you are now presiding as governor."

Certain of defeat, Armijo dispersed his troops, packed abruptly, and bolted for Mexico. On August 19, Kearny marched his army of nearly seventeen hundred men into Santa Fe, meeting almost no opposition. The governor's office, hastily emptied of Armijo's personal effects, held a surprise: Armijo had left the ears of five Texans tacked to the wall, tokens of a previous army's failed attempt to conquer New Mexico.

In a separate proclamation to the people of New Mexico, Kearny declared: "The undersigned has instructions from his government to respect the religious institutions of

GRAVE, TRUCHAS

New Mexico—to protect the property of the church—to cause the worship of those belonging to it to be undisturbed and their religious rights in the amplest manner preserved to them—also to protect the persons and property of all quiet and peaceable inhabitants within its boundaries."

"Our men just left the front and went home," Cathy says, her voice filled with disappointment. "Their place was to protect the women. I guess they were right to worry. People claim these blue eyes you see around here are because we are pure Castilians from Spain. Oh, no." She wags an accusing finger and smiles. "Some of those guys from Kearny's army jumped the fence."

The initial entry into New Mexico was counted as an easy victory for the Army of the West. But it would produce bitterness and difficulties that would endure for years. Reportedly, Kearny's American soldiers were rowdy men who drank heavily and antagonized the local women; their behavior inspired resentment and opposition. The Hispanics waited, their bitterness rising, and took advantage of each opportunity for revenge as it presented itself. An uprising in Mora left eight soldiers dead, and another in Taos brought down six more. Pockets of that lingering malice exist to this day.

Cathy's particular point of view on local culture developed in part from her having spent a number of years away from northern New Mexico. She returned, renewed her ties to her family, and began working as a teacher. She had a goal. She hoped her efforts would help improve the quality of life in the valley without sacrificing local customs and traditions. Strongest among those customs were the desire to live near the land, to honor the bonds of family, and to maintain strong religious ties.

"I remember when I realized how much there was to our heritage. Shortly after I came back to the valley a relative of my dad's died up in Dixon and my *tia,* my aunt, said, 'Come on, let's go to the funeral.' I mean, funerals are a big deal around here, right?

"I was standing outside the church when one of the local men walks up and says, 'Who are you?'

"'Cathy Berryhill.'

"'What were you before you were Berryhill?'

"'Martínez.'

MASTER WEAVER, MEDENALES

"'What Martínez? From where?'

"'From here. My dad's from right here in Dixon.'

"'Who is your dad?'

"All I had to do was mention his name and the man knew him—as well as my grandpa and my great-grandfather and all my *tíos* and my cousins. It's like I was suddenly plugged back into the culture. It was so graphic. I know people who go to psychiatrists and get involved with encounter groups to find their identity. All I had to do was to go to my *tío* Procopio's funeral to be reminded of mine. It said: *This is where you belong.* I was home."

I am skeptical. Does her eagerness stem partially from guilt? She left the valley to attend school. She married an Anglo. She stayed away for a decade. Then she returned, having acquired a certain sophistication, only to find that this increased her concern about her native culture. She realized how unique it was, and how fragile. The problems she faced in trying to maintain it against the encroachment of the modern world—the lack of confidence and skills in the people—were compounded by history. They reflected the accelerated pace of the times—the intrusion of Los Alamos, for example— and a new economic system that had gradually displaced the trading and bartering that governed local commerce during the previous centuries.

According to Cathy, the culture she slipped back into is currently in decline. Part of the cause, she maintains, is an apathetic younger generation. "Our kids are losing focus on all the old things, the things that make us special. They are no longer exposed to the old people. That's a vital connection and they're not making it."

"The sins of the fathers—"

"Exactly. We are probably the last generation whose grandparents never spoke English," she says. "My grandmother used to say: 'Why should I learn English? You need to learn Spanish.' She was always throwing disparaging remarks in our direction, trying to remind us who we were. She was right, of course.

"We are so far from our roots now that it's pathetic. Our children are not even bilingual. Our culture used to be based on protocol and respect. As kids we were taught the amenities: *Don't you ever walk into a room without greeting everyone who is older than yourself. You ask them how they are.* I find those same instructions coming out of my mouth to my kids." She shakes her forefinger and speaks in imitation of herself. "'You go say hi to your *tia.*'" She smiles. "And they do. My brothers and my sister and I were raised to be respectful to people, very *gente,* very polite. When people came to visit, we were expected to sit down in the living room, stay put, shut up, and not make pests of ourselves. That idea has carried over in our families. It's a lingering thing in the culture, like an appendix from a time long gone. But it is disappearing.

"We've stripped down our heritage and picked at it until all we have left are threads of that incredible culture we were born into. The weaving, the farming, the livestock, all the stuff that lay at the heart of our lives and enriched it in so many ways are almost gone. Some of the arts have been revived, true, but that's partly because of the Anglos and the tourists—the wrong reasons. When you see the people in Espanola and they seem lost, with no place to go, it's because they *are* lost and literally do have no place to go. They're trapped between two worlds—your world and what used to be ours.

"There's been progress—I think that's what we call it—but there are still a lot of people who live in that old world, which is so different from the new world brought in by the Anglos."

"What do you mean by the 'old world'?"

"A different place, with a different set of rules," she replies. "I was taught, for instance, that the man is the head of the house and respect is given to the man based on his position—maybe not because he is a wonderful person or anything, but you give respect to a man because he is a man."

"What I hear you saying is that in this society Hispanic women are under the thumb of men."

"It is more complicated than that. I am controlled by not only my husband but my uncles, too, and my aunts, and my mom and my kids. That's the way it's always been with Hispanic women."

Contrary to what Cathy is saying, the local women continue to form a strong hub of family life. Whole families wheel around them. The women hold things together. I see examples every day—in the village, in the workplace. With this in mind, I challenge her statement.

"All right," she recants. "We are strong. We were raised to be strong. We've always canned; we've always dried fruit; we've always picked chile and made ristras. And we still do it. Why? Because we still have little old ladies who make sure that we do it. I'm one. I make my kids do some of that stuff. Why? Because we need to keep it alive. No matter what we've done or where we've been, a lot of us still find it hard to make the leap from the old world to this new world."

I press her again about the 'old world.' What does she mean?

"I mean the practices and traditions that've made us who we are. Early in my life, I learned the feel of the *masa* we make tortillas from. I knew when it was ready to put on the stove. I could make tortillas without even thinking. They were part of the information I carried inside of me."

A young female student approaching from the next building catches Cathy's eye. The girl's heart-shaped face is ablaze with makeup and her skin-tight jeans hug her small, sexy figure. She wears her hair teased up so it rises in a high lacquered wave in front and cascades down her back. Cathy shakes her head and laughs. "I've got a theory about these girls with the big hair," she says. "They're beautiful. They're brassy and they're bold and, you know what, they're sensuous and they're sexy. Like that one. Look. Walking around with her pants caught right up in her butt. She's beautiful, and she's saying, 'This is me. If you don't like it, tough shit.' I think that's just great."

"How does this girl fit into the 'old world' you keep mentioning?"

"She fits," Cathy insists. "Except she's not the way we used to be. When I was growing up, Hispanic women used to be modest. My *tias* never wore pants, always dresses that had sleeves. They were conscious of being known as 'good' women, right? But these girls are different. Some people say it comes from a low self-esteem—where the only thing you really have for sure is your body. But, hey, eighteen-year-old bodies are wonderful. Everything is still where it's supposed to be." She laughs.

"No," she says, serious again, "these girls are very much aware of the world and their possibilities in it and they're getting a lot of strokes from their peer group. These are real

Chicano women, brassy and bold." She emphasizes the Chicano, perhaps alluding to the on-again-off-again revolution. "We grew up feeling we weren't as good as the gringo girls. They were the class presidents; they made the national honor society; they had money to buy neat clothes. We had to make our own. We were always behind the times. These girls today are different."

Leaving the college to have lunch, we slip into the traffic on the Chama highway. Espanola is famous for its cars and notorious for its unpredictable drivers. We are caught in a slowdown caused by a pair of lowriders. Crawling side by side, they shout to each other as they bounce along. One, a gray Coupe de Ville, scrapes over a rough spot and a flurry of sparks flies up from its undercarriage. The driver of the other, his greased down hair in a net and a Dizzy Gillespie goatee on his lower lip, clutches the chromed chain-link steering wheel of his white Thunderbird. His car beetles along, shuddering as it hits a pothole. He hits a lever and suddenly the body rises up on its hydraulic suspension. The car leaps ahead and goes snorting toward the bridge. Once again, the traffic begins to flow.

Espanola's car culture has achieved national attention. The local lowriders were recently featured on MTV and are the subject of an opera. One car was shipped to Washington, D.C., to become part of the permanent collection of the Smithsonian Institution. Working with steel and lacquer, the lowriders are unlikely artists emerging from the local body shops instead of the university fine arts programs. They pour their ingenuity into a variety of vehicles. They lower and customize Buicks, Chevys, Fords, turning them into sleek tubs barely able to clear the pavement. They fit out their 4 × 4s, the "highriders," with huge tires and jack them up so high on extended suspension systems that it takes a ladder to reach the running board. The most recent craze has been to add custom camper tops to sleek Japanese mini-pickups, creating awesome sound chambers fitted with built-in mega-boom-box music systems powerful enough to rattle the store windows along Riverside Drive.

But if the tricked-out cars with their altered features represent an outlet for creative expression, they are also evidence of the restlessness that seethes in the valley. On summer evenings and weekend afternoons, the cruisers circle the Sonic Drive-in and collect

EL PUEBLO STATE BANK, ESPANOLA

FASHION STORE, ESPANOLA

in the parking lot outside the old Furr's store. They hang out, suck on joints, and drink beer until a city police car creeps among them and forces them back into the traffic.

Cathy pauses in the parking lot outside Angelina's Restaurant. "What we once had here was a life based on gentleness. Our men had pride." She bites her lip. Her eyes shine with a sudden rush of tears that she quickly swallows.

"I don't see that gentleness you keep bringing up," I argue. "This area has a history of violence. It started with the early Spaniards abusing the Indians. Violence is committed within families. I read about it every week. Now people tell me Espanola is the mass-murder capital of the United States."

"Yes, and I think that's because our traditions are dying," she replies. "People don't know anymore how to act. I get a little emotional when I see our boys. They go out and get drunk; their arms are scarred with needle marks. They are no longer proud of what they do—because their lives are in limbo. There used to be a time when men had pride in the crops they raised, the work they did. The men were horsemen. San Juan de los Caballeros, you know, horse people, gentlemen." She lifts her head proudly. "They were real men with a real desire to do things. Getting up in the _madrugada,_ that was something you did, you got up early in the morning and you worked the earth. There was this great satisfaction you got from owning property and working with your own animals. The land meant everything. Your roots were in the land, you worked that land, and you were proud of the things you grew. That's the way you supported your family.

"But it's not like that anymore. In just how many generations? Two? Three?" She shakes her head sadly. "Back then, the life was based on agriculture. That's what we are, an agriculturally oriented society. Now we find ourselves surrounded by technology, Los Alamos. I hear people saying Hispanics can't think, they can't do math, they can't do science." The idea makes her indignant. "Of course we can't. Why should we just naturally know that? We have no history of those things. Until this generation, you couldn't ask your parents for help in higher sciences. They didn't know what you were talking about. It's like you take this whole group of people who were close to the soil for generations and you expect them to suddenly be able to handle intellectual pursuits, to talk and act in a way that is totally foreign to them. How could they? How could anyone?

"The kids at the college write papers and their English teachers, my colleagues, say to them, 'You don't know how to think.' It's like telling them what they have is not valuable. Well, I think the stuff they have inside is valuable."

In her own classes, Cathy admonishes her students to reach into their lives and treat what they find with pride. "What most teachers expect these kids to write is impossible for them. I ask for something else: What is a day you'll never forget? They write: 'The Day My Grandpa Died'; 'The Day My Dad Died'; 'The Day I Had My Kid.' Those are important moments in their lives. I understand that; I appreciate it. But they move into another class and they are asked to write on a similar theme and the paper comes back with the remark written on it: *This is colloquial*. Okay, so it is colloquial, but it's what they feel and those feelings are important."

"'I want something from your heart,' the teachers tell the kids. But when the kids write from the heart, those same teachers turn around and say, 'Wait a minute, this isn't the heart I want. Your heart isn't good enough. How come you don't have an Anglo heart? How come you don't have a heart that thinks these wonderful abstract and mystical thoughts?' There is no way you can tell that kind of teacher how roasting and peeling a bag of chile is important because it brings your family together, that you associate those moments with that smell and all the activities around it. So what these kids get in school are too many double messages from teachers who say, in effect: you came to school but you are still not good enough. You might as well go back to Petaca and stay there — on welfare."

Cathy is worked up. She touches her chest with her flattened palm. She would like to laugh it off, but she can't. "Come on," she says, "let's go in and eat."

Angelina's was once owned by the local *patrón*, Emilio Naranjo. The story is that when he wanted out of the business he let it pass into the hands of his cook. True or not, the restaurant is more popular than it ever was. Each booth in the interior is modeled on a piece of local architecture — the jail, the church, the bank. The decor is camp but the food is genuine, like the New Mexican food at Joanne's, Matilda's, Red's, the Rio Grande Cafe. In a different class are Anthony's at the Delta and El Paragua, places with elegant decor, a smooth ambience, and reputations that reach beyond New Mexico.

As soon as the waitress has taken our order, Cathy leans across the table and says, "After teaching in the schools here, I realize what an amazing person my dad was. He was in the crossover generation. We grew up with electricity in our homes, but he had wood fires and candles. Not that his generation ever felt deprived. His father was a meticulous man, a perfectionist. He was a farmer and a wood person. He gathered wood and sold it in Taos during the fall and winter. His orchard was always meticulous. I mean, everything my grandfather did he did very meticulously.

"My dad's mother died very young, thirty-one or thirty-two. His dad, my grandfather, married again and there was some conflict with the stepmother. What do they call them now, blended families? But like my mother's father my father's father also saw to it that his children were educated. They went to the Presbyterian Mission School in Dixon and then to the Menaul School in Albuquerque. He went on to business school. Somebody told him there were jobs in Washington, D.C., so he went. While he was there, he graduated from the University of Maryland. What an incredible amount of courage he had to have to just leave this area and go do something else."

"You left," I point out.

"Yes, but I had his example. We do go away," she says, "but we never really leave—not totally. The valley goes along with us. We're all over the place. They call us the *manitos* of northern New Mexico, the *manito* nation. *Hermanitos*, little brothers, literally. Listen for it, you'll hear it. *Hey, manito, como?* You can always find the *manito* nation—in Utah, in California, Chicago, so many places. They left in World War II to become Rosie the Riveter and work on the war machine. Some never came back. Wherever they were they held on to the piece of the *manito* nation they'd taken with them."

Cathy grew up in a household in which roles were clearly defined. She sees it as an extension of the culture. "In those days, the home was the realm of the mother," she says. "There was none of this business of the dad coming home to vacuum and mop. No, the fields were the realm of the father—except in the winter when he came in and did weaving."

"How does this fit with the idea of liberation?"

"Liberation—" The word stops her.

"For women."

"Liberation has done some bad things for women. We're no longer the queen of anything." She laughs. "Now we're the slave of everybody. But there was a time when the mother was the queen of the home."

"Was that true in your home?"

"Yes. My mother is really something." She smiles. "When she started school, she didn't even know English. But she went all the way through school and then she, too, went to D.C. and got a job. She and my dad got together there. Imagine! Two people from this little valley meeting each other in D.C. See how it works? The *manitos* always find each other."

The waitress brings the food, cautioning that the plates are hot. Cathy tastes her enchilada and is silent for a moment. "My mom was probably one of the first generations of working women from Espanola. She had a job in the Forest Service and I think she found being away from the house very frustrating. She lived in two worlds, but I think she melded them nicely. Because of her job we all had to work hard. We had to keep up a garden, we had to do canning, help with the cooking."

"Do you think the fact that she left home and worked contributed to a breakdown of the culture in your home?"

"Not really. We spoke Spanish. Not totally. She and my dad did. But we all learned to speak it. One great-aunt lived with us for a while and my aunt Kate lived with us. So did my dad's stepmother. All Spanish-speaking. I learned that the extended family, which is what this culture is based on, can give kids a real sense of identity. I'll tell you why. If your parents are mad at you and you're not getting along with them, one of the other people around will help you and that can do a lot for your sense of identity.

"I really get upset when I hear these Anglo ladies say, 'I never leave my kids with a baby-sitter,' and they are so proud of it. I think, 'Well that's really great, lady, but you are not the only person who can put valuable things into your child.' I don't care who it is, grandpas, grandmas, *tias*, and uncles. Who cares if that grandpa is weird? The kids're going to remember how he used to be able to spit between those two crooked teeth of his or they're going to remember how Grandma had that special old-lady smell and all those other things that make people unique. They are going to realize that they belong, that they fit in, and that people other than their parents care about them."

Outside the restaurant we talk and observe the flow of lunchtime traffic. At a stand in the next lot a man is roasting chiles. He stands at a cylinder made of wire mesh, turning it slowly over a gas burner, tumbling the green chiles until their skins turn black and begin to blister. His wife fishes out the pods so they can cool. The pungent smell, borne on the breeze, reaches us. Cathy sniffs and closes her eyes. "That is reason enough to be in this valley."

"You are a teacher," I say, bringing the conversation back to an earlier point. "Is it fair to assume that education is the solution?"

"My great-grandfather on my mother's side, who must have been alive shortly after Kearny came in through the Las Vegas pass, believed education was the only way out."

Her forebears, however, were in the minority. There was a small movement toward improved education for Hispanics in New Mexico, led by the controversial Taos priest Padre Martínez. But his views were not shared by the majority of northern New Mexicans. Schools were considered a luxury to most people and a sacrifice to many others who depended on their young sons to help in the fields and who viewed the classroom as a drain on their essential labor force.

"School was an exciting thing for my family," Cathy continues. "My mom said that one of the neatest things that ever happened to her was going to meet her sisters when they were coming home after boarding the year at school. It was a two-day trip from Chimayo to Santa Fe. Her dad would go and get them when it was time to come home for summer vacation. Her mother would have everything cleaned and ironed. My mother would walk from their house in Chimayo all the way down to the river up near Potrero and watch for the wagon to come up over the hill. She knew her father would have supplies and gifts.

"Everybody in my mom's family graduated from high school and several went on to get college degrees."

"Did that make it difficult to continue the old ways?"

"My family never gave them up," she says. "The summer my husband, Don, and I came back to New Mexico, my uncle decided he was going to plant chile on a commercial basis. He had these big fields of chile and we all got excited. For what reason, I don't know, because we weren't going to make any money from it. It was his chile crop. But everybody took a personal interest in it—because we were family. We would all go help him hoe his chiles. Well, that chile grew to be the nicest crop you ever saw. It was beautiful. Then one night he got robbed. That was awful. I can laugh about it now, but at the time it was so tragic. Boy, the *tías* were out there the next day. We marshalled forces and picked all that chile before anybody else could hit it again.

"That's how we had learned to live. When we were kids we used to gather at my grandma's house to work. Whatever the project of the moment was, we would all do it together. The women would make the food and the men would go out and work. Then my grandma died. And after that nothing was the same. That was the big break. When her generation died, things came to an end. Now we live in homes in suburbia or whatever. It's all different. But as long as my grandmother's generation was alive, life continued just as it had for a long time."

LOS VIEJOS, ALCALDE

A Question of History

History can clarify the origins of many of our
phantasms, but it cannot dissipate them. We must
confront them ourselves. . . . We are the only persons
who can answer the questions asked us by reality
and our own being.

OCTAVIO PAZ

The call Hilario Romero took just after I walked into his office has lasted longer than he expected, a sentiment he conveys with a helpless shrug. He stands out of his chair, holding the receiver against his ear with his shoulder and leafs through a stack of mail. Hilario is trim and fit; he has a runner's body. He wears jeans, a denim shirt, and slip-on shoes. He turns and sits again. Bored. The tip of his ballpoint pen leaves a series of doodles across the face of the phone book.

The office is cluttered with stacks of correspondence, professional journals, research materials, papers in progress. Bookshelves line three walls; the volumes, well used, their pages flagged with pink and yellow slips, are shelved two deep, with an overflow in boxes on the floor, clear indications of a bookish person with an insatiable curiosity.

Hilario, a working historian and a custodian of local culture, makes it his business to keep the sources within grasp. During an earlier conversation, he admitted that he had an ax to grind, adding that there were a few things about the valley I ought to understand. It is a point I will not argue. I am here to listen and learn.

The call finally finished, he hangs up and swivels his chair to face me. His eyes are quick and intense, the air in the room suddenly charged with his energy. Before the phone rang, I asked him to place the Espanola Valley somewhere along a continuum of Southwest history. I am prepared to rephrase the question but he is ready with an answer. "If you consider the thousands of years of Native American history that exists here," he begins in sweeping fashion, "the Espanola Valley is a very important place in history. The Pueblo Indians had lived here for centuries before the Spanish showed up. Their system of life was well organized. They produced corn, beans, squash, and chile and they hunted wild game. Survival here wasn't easy, but they managed.

"When the colonizers came, the Indians had already established sophisticated irrigation practices. They studied the heavens and measured the movements of the sun, moon, and stars, reading them as their ancestors the Anasazi and Mogollon had done before them. They had a unique system of life that was in balance with their environment. If you took something, you made sure you gave something back. Their lives were governed by that incredible harmony. North, Central, and South America were all one big island, with communication and trade between the tribes. They traveled and there was a sense of continuity."

The Spaniards considered the Indians savages and deplored their heathen practices. They failed to look to the Pueblos as a source of wisdom. The reason for this, Hilario believes, was the arrogance of the written word. "All the reporting was done by Oñate and his chroniclers," he says. "Everything we know came from the European perspective. The Spaniards did nothing to understand the Indian people. They did not consider that the Indians might have a point of view. They lived by the written word. If it's written, it's true, right?"

He leans forward to drive home his point. "The Indian people had been taught the oral tradition. To this day, their oral history is very accurate. These tales get told over and over until they are embedded in the minds and lives of the people. Let's face it, the greatest computer in the world is the human mind. Those people relied on their computers more than we do today. Now we have what I call mind masturbation. We let machines do everything for us. Back then they had to internalize all this information and compute it. Because it was the information they had to have in order to live to the next day. It was their key to survival."

The Spaniards disregarded the fact that the Indians' concerns went beyond the immediate need of food and shelter. They failed to recognize that there was real value in what the Indians studied in the secrecy of the kiva and what they knew about living on the land. "The Pueblos and their ancestors acknowledged celestial happenings. One important event in their oral history was sighting the Crab Nebula, the supernova. That is really important, because in Europe people either ignored it or they called it superstition—anything not to acknowledge it. It was still the Dark Ages in Europe. Those people were eating rats. They attributed the whole appearance of the supernova to paganism and fantasy.

"Here it was different. All Native Americans related to that phenomenon," Hilario says. "It showed their sophistication and their knowledge of the world around them. That should never be forgotten. But it is. Or it was never acknowledged. So, what has changed?" He shrugs. "If you want a weather forecast for New Mexico today you call Howard Morgan at KOAT-TV in Albuquerque, even though there are better forecasters at the pueblos. They've been around a long time. Howard Morgan uses computers to watch his weather. In New Mexico none of the stations get a forecast right, because New Mexico is unique. We have seven life zones out of eight, elevations ranging from two thousand feet all the way up to thirteen thousand. There is nothing uniform you can say about the state of New Mexico—geographically, historically, or any other way. So, if you want an accurate forecast you go to the *viejitos* who have been farming this land for a long time or you go to the Pueblos. They are always watching. If something new's going to happen in the sky they'll be aware of it."

I mention that among injustices the Europeans showed toward the native people was their refusal to consider the authenticity of their beliefs. Insecurity went hand in hand with the Christian arrogance of the Spaniards. They looked at the natives with horror and fear, unable to see anything except that the Indians had not risen to a level of belief that included Jesus Christ and the church in Rome.

"It's true," Hilario agrees, and he takes the idea a step further. "The Europeans could not conceive of the Indian world. The Indians pointed out their sacred mountains and the Spaniards scoffed, 'No, that mountain does not have a purpose. Except if you go up there and hunt and bring back something to eat.' The Indians insisted there was a spirit in the mountain. They had shrines all over the hills to mark out their spiritual space; these were altars where they made offerings to their gods. Most of them are gone now. People destroyed them. The Indian shrines had to be hidden, internalized."

Nature, the land, the core of the Pueblos' universe, was the axle around which all ceremonial life revolved. Their lives had been continuously shaped by the cosmos and they were neither bewildered by its design nor afraid of its vast mysteries. They were only mindful at all times of its omnipotence.

"The Franciscan priests were a little better than the other Spaniards and Mexicans," Hilario allows. "Even though they were scared, they were fascinated. My God, you can almost hear them," he says, leaping from his chair, pantomiming their fear. " 'We are among heathens! These people don't believe in Christ! How could they have possibly survived all these years without Christ?' " He pauses to laugh. He sits again, his chair creaking.

"But these guys, these priests, wrote detail," he says. "That is their saving grace, so to speak, they recorded data, and this has helped us to understand."

"To understand the Native Americans or the Spaniards?"

"Probably more about the Spaniards," he grants, his face creasing into a smile. "But they talked about the kivas and the ceremonies. The Pueblo people were very open with the Spaniards. Mainly because they had never seen anything like the conquistadors. It was as if a spaceship had come down." He spreads his hands. "How would we relate to aliens? If they were friendly, we'd be open and share our things with them—because we were afraid. The Indians did and the Spaniards took advantage of it. They were bigoted and narrow-minded and in the end they turned on the Indians. They violated their trust."

"Don't you think the Native Americans were more than a little puzzled by the European God?" I suggest. "After all the variety they were accustomed to in their spiritual lives, he must have seemed grossly underpowered."

SHRINE, THE RIO GRANDE NEAR CHAMITA

TRUCHAS

SANTERO, ESPANOLA

"Listen," Hilario replies, "just because I am related to most of them in some way, I refuse to make excuses for the Spaniards. They were cruel. To them the only good Indian was a dead Indian. Except that they believed an enslaved Indian was better than a dead Indian because you could get something out of him. And they worked them like dogs.

"The Spaniards were as vindictive as they were authoritarian," Hilario says, offering as an example one of the most heinous assaults in the history of the Southwest. "Oñate attacked the people at Acoma after they had wounded his brother and killed some of his soldiers. He captured them and cut off the feet of their warriors." He rolls his chair to a bookshelf to get a volume he thinks will support his statement. He doesn't find it, shrugs, and goes on. "The Acomas have never forgotten. That incident is logged in their oral tradition. I have friends at Acoma. When I go out there and my friends take me to meet their families, I see the whole history of Oñate's betrayal in their eyes. Here is this Spaniard, those looks are saying. What does he want from us?"

He leaps on ahead. "The Spanish *adelantados* had no more power than General Kearny. Which is a comparison I like. This territory saw the worst of them. Stephen W. Kearny, representing the United States, came out here and said, in effect, 'Now you're all going to take the oath of allegiance.' Well, bullshit!" Hilario's feet come off his chair onto the floor with a bang. "Kearny was totally out of order. That takes an act of Congress. To make matters worse, at the end of the skirmishes he held treason trials in Taos." He pauses, incredulous. "How can you have treason trials in an occupied territory?" He lets the words ring. "Kearny did. He put people on the gallows. I know descendants of those people and they have not forgotten. Their question is: 'How could they hang my great-great-grandpa for treason against the United States when he wasn't even a citizen of the United States? He was defending his country.'"

Little wonder the local people drew into themselves, taking refuge in their villages, in their isolation. First came the Spanish against the native people. Then the United States, its policy to wipe out Native Americans already in place, made a stand against both the Native Americans and the Spanish in New Mexico.

"Think of what they learned," Hilario says. "There are individuals in this valley, Native Americans who are trilingual and tricultural. They are involved with the food, the weaving, the pottery, the religion, the dances, all the things that make us unique. Those are their tools. Some Pueblo Indians have that unique triple identity—especially the older generation. They speak Spanish, Tewa, and English. They have three identity caps and they put on those caps when they are around certain people. They're able to move from one to another with complete ease because their core identity was established early and had been kept intact throughout."

"But that must also create problems." I am thinking of a kind of cultural schizophrenia, a floating identity without a center.

"The biggest problem"—and here he raises a cautioning finger—"is that they are losing the language. The kids aren't learning it and, as a result, they are having problems. They need their tongue to have a solid identity with their culture."

"Is it only the children?" I ask. "What about the earlier generation that was encouraged, or, as some say, *forced* to leave by government programs?"

"Yes, you see it with the ones who left the pueblo to find a job or to get college degrees. When I worked for the Eight Northern Pueblos, I saw them. It was like they were trying to implant all the things they'd learned from the Anglos into their tribe. The tribe said, 'Hey, wait a minute, you used to be in the kiva and you used to dance, but you haven't done any of those things for a long time. Now you've got to start from scratch and relearn the movement of this pueblo. Just because you have management skills doesn't mean we're gonna let you run the tribe.'

"That's one reason most Indians prefer to stay on the reservation or to move out totally, instead of moving into the nearest small community. They tend to go to Albuquerque or somewhere else where they won't be identified as being outside of the tribe."

"I get the feeling that you think the Native Americans will always be outsiders."

"They *are* outsiders," he states. "No doubt about it. Both the Indian and Hispano cultures in northern New Mexico are non-Western entities. We don't base our philosophies on Aristotelian theory or what Socrates had to say. We have learned about them, those of us who have become educated. But life in this area is really attuned to a philosophy that is non-Western. It comes from the Pueblos. It comes from the isolation. It comes from the local Catholic Church."

POTTER, SAN ILDEFONSO

"Are you telling me you would separate what you call the local Catholic Church from the larger church?"

"Absolutely," he insists. "The Catholic Church in New Mexico is completely different from the Roman Catholic Church. There is no comparison. It was obvious how different we were when Jean-Baptiste Lamy came in 1850."

Again his voice is charged, bitter. Lamy, the French priest brought to New Mexico in the nineteenth century and celebrated by Willa Cather and others, has been a source of contention among Hispanics for over a century. Cather painted a poignant portrait but Hilario feels her sources were unfairly limited to the Lamy myth, largely self-conceived. "Real resentment exists in this area about what that man did," he says of Lamy, who became archbishop in 1875. "Every time I see that statue of him up in front of the French Cathedral in Santa Fe, I say the person who belongs up there is Padre Antonio José Martínez. And the old *parroquia* should still be there. That new building really sends out a message. It's like a big neon sign saying: 'Hey, we reformed your church.' "

Padre Martínez's name is surrounded by controversy. Born in Rio Arriba County in 1793, Antonio José Martínez lost his wife and child while he was still a young man. The experience turned him toward the priesthood. He studied in Durango, Mexico, was ordained, and then returned to take over the church at Taos. He was a man of great energy and vision, one dedicated to his people. At his own expense, he started a school; he bought a press, the first in New Mexico, and printed a newspaper, pamphlets, and church tracts. He became a hero to his people. Rumors were voiced concerning his conduct and there was no little jealousy about the popularity and power he enjoyed within the Hispanic community.

Bishop Lamy defrocked him. But his parishioners did not abandon him. For another eleven years, until he died, they flocked to his church to hear him say Mass.

"I did my master's thesis on Padre Antonio José Martínez," Hilario says, the syllables of the name sliding easily off his tongue. "It was the first of its kind. I used every original document that I could find on Martínez. I put together the largest single collection, even larger than his family's."

Writing this thesis put the finishing touches on Hilario's own formal education and taught him a lesson in the methods of racism.

"I was working on this at the same time Paul Horgan was writing his work on Lamy. There were five documents missing from the church archives that to this date, as far as I know, are still in the hands of Paul Horgan. During my research I kept looking for certain key documents that seemed to have disappeared and sure enough they show up in the footnotes to Horgan's book. I wrote Horgan about it and my letters are still unanswered. Fray Angelico Chavez had allowed this guy to take those original documents." (Paul Horgan died in 1989.)

The injustices meted out to Padre Martínez make Hilario boil. "In the same way a general cannot administer the oath of office to those he conquers—like General Kearny tried to do in Las Vegas—Lamy tried to excommunicate Padre Martínez. You don't do that without the Holy See. The Holy See wouldn't have much to do with Lamy or his cohorts. Padre Martínez was never officially excommunicated. He was an incredible man with enormous vision and understanding. He knew canon law better than anybody of his time in the United States. He wrote fifty or sixty books—on everything from _la lingua Castellana_ to politics. He liked to say the United States was like a donkey."

Hilario refers to a statement quoted in a book written by Pedro Sánchez about Padre Martínez. "The American government resembles a burro; but on this burro lawyers will ride, not priests."

"Padre Martínez knew U.S. history backwards and forwards. He had corresponded with Daniel Webster. He was brilliant."

Hilario shakes his head. "I can't believe what Willa Cather and Paul Horgan tried to do to him. They didn't even take time to really find out who he was. They wrote their books and butchered the hell out of local history and the good name of Padre Martínez. Horgan used no documentation other than Lamy's word. Padre Martínez was this, he said, and Padre Gallegos was that. All accusations but no proof."

Hilario pauses.

"What was the difference between the Roman church and the local church—Lamy and Martínez?"

"One of the differences," he says, "is that we were abandoned by Rome and left to make it on our own for years. That bred bitterness and resentment. The *penitentes* and others did all they could to keep the church alive. There has never been a complete reconciliation.

"I learned the difference between the Roman church and the New Mexican church," he continues. "I went to a school run by Dominican nuns. They were either Irish or German, from Baltimore. They would have had a much harder time had they not been given incredible authority. That authority had a very negative effect upon the people here— especially the children. Lucky for me, my grandmother didn't put up with it. When anything happened she went over there and knocked on the door and gave them hell. A couple of them spoke Spanish and she always knew where to find them. They kept saying, 'We're all Catholic, we're all God's children.' But I know that inside they thought differently."

"Was your entire early education in the Catholic system?"

"I said I went to the Catholic school," he corrects, his eyes fastening on mine as he makes his point. "My education is something else. From the time I was five years old, I was reared on my grandfather's knee. No school in the world can give you that kind of education. He talked about the family, about the local history, the importance of the soil. My grandmothers also educated me. They didn't speak a word of English. They'd never been to school. But they were my real educators. They gave me the wisdom to grow up fast. Under their tutelage I matured much sooner than my brother and sister, who had learned to go with the flow. I went against it. Maybe that's part of it. They were the straight-A students. They got the scholarships but I'm the one who ended up with all the degrees. That influence of my grandparents was really strong. When I lost them I was a wreck. I just didn't want them to die. I had too much invested in them.

"One grandmother lived with us all the time," he recalls. Then he adds with emphasis: "Which is an important factor in my life. My grandmother was my roommate. My brother went off to college and my grandmother moved into my room. And people didn't understand that. "I mean, my high school buddies would come into my room and say, 'Hey, who sleeps in that bed, your brother?'

Deer Dance, San Juan Pueblo

"I'd say, 'No, he's in college. It's my grandmother.'

"'Your grandmother sleeps in that bed?' they'd say. 'You're sleeping in the same room with your grandmother?'

"You could see their minds working on that one: What the hell is going on here? To me it was no big deal."

"Does that kind of thing go on as much now?"

He shakes his head. "Not anymore. These days even the elderly care centers in the valley have more Hispanos. There didn't used to be any. They were all taken care of by the families.

"I'm partial to the old people," he explains. "They invested their lives and today we could reap the benefits of what they had to go through. And I mean they went through shit. Talk about pride swallowing. I never quite had to do that. When I had to deal with racism, I confronted it."

"Today people don't think of racism in New Mexico."

"Anglos don't," he corrects. "I used to be a bilingual teacher-trainer in some isolated programs in the Carlsbad-Roswell area down there in the bottom of the state. The first time I showed up, those Anglo teachers would be waiting for me with little daggers in their eyes. It was like they were saying, I dare you to sensitize me. And I just niced them to death and we got it done. They were not purely within their hearts hateful, racist people. It was just a facade they had to put up, maybe for protective reasons.

"The ones I really worry about are the covert racists. The ones who say, 'Hey, bro, Hispanos are wonderful.' Then when a real issue comes up, they slip behind the scenes and start sticking pins in their little voodoo doll."

I ask if he's doing anything to prepare his own children for the kind of experiences he went through.

"I am trying to expose my children to the core of their culture. I tell them, 'This is you and this is your environment.' I talk to them about the local arts and go with them to the dances at the pueblos and at fiestas. I tell them they should feel good about what they have, and once they know that then they can go out and see the rest of the world. With that base they can do what they want. In schools, I tell kids, 'If you want to learn about your upbringing and your heritage, find your grandpa and sit on his lap and listen. And if that grandpa doesn't know anything then you go find his brother or sister and if you don't get anything from them then you go find somebody in the community.'"

"I keep hearing that the culture is being lost."

"In this valley, there is a surprisingly significant amount still intact. The continuity of culture and the strength of the culture has always dominated the area. There is still a *rico patrón* system in Espanola. The rich patron has lasted longer here than in Santa Fe, which has been taken over by gringo land developers such as Gerald Peters, a different kind of *patrón*. The traditional *patrón* took care of the families, which included their friends. The gringo developer *patrón*, from the new culture, takes care of himself.

"In Espanola and Rio Arriba County, the acknowledged *patrón* is Emilio Naranjo. Emilio is a continuation of something out of the past," Hilario says. "There was an Emilio Naranjo before Emilio Naranjo. There was another one like him before that and before that. Now, that's starting to change. Emilio still has control of the county, but he is losing that power. When he is gone there's going to be a change.

"The valley is opening up, like it or not. It's slow. The Hispanos here live in two worlds—past and present. They're still tied to their families. They keep closing the door on newcomers. Like the Indians, they have lost the openness they used to have. They've been burned too many times."

I ask if the new plaza being planned for Espanola will rekindle the unity.

"The new plaza," he says, "is a big joke. You can't buy culture. The mayor and his henchmen are forgetting who we are. They're doing it the way gringos do it. Think of Georgetown and all those places where you sell your history through a T-shirt shop. My mother's family is from Santa Cruz de la Cañada, and that is why I am so against the Espanola plaza and the whole effort to connect Oñate with Espanola. Originally, this was Santa Clara and San Juan land. Period. Espanola was only a railroad stop. A few of what we now call land developers got together with a few of the *patróns* and made some wheels and deals and managed to develop a community out of this Indian land. Santa Cruz de la Cañada was the center of government up here from 1695 to the present century. That's where the plaza was and where it should be today."

In the confusion of the twentieth century, the focus of life in the valley changed. Since the colonization, the Catholic Church had formed the center of each community. Now that has shifted. The Methodists came in during the last century, and the Presbyterians, and more recently Mormons and the fire-and-brimstone people, the fundamentalists, have begun to claim the conservatives. They each established their little islands, fortified themselves, and they have continued to grow, subverting Catholic power, breaking up old allegiances.

"Those people do things differently," Hilario goes on. "The Anglos and others don't mind living in an adobe house as long as it is an uptown adobe. They wall themselves in and plant all that Kentucky bluegrass until they are separate from the community. They make some noise but they aren't a threat."

I ask him about the people who insist on claiming the blood of Oñate and the Spaniards.

"It is embarrassing to some of them to think that they might not be a descendant," he says, with a shake of his head. "If you're not related to Oñate, how can you be great, right? How can you be anybody? I remember my *tio* Juan Rival. He would be about a hundred years old today. He always called himself Spanish. I said, 'Listen, *tio*, the Anglos gave that term to you back when they decided to put you on their census. They said you're Spanish-American, which is more acceptable than being a Mexican.' Well, he didn't want to hear that. If you were a Mexican you were somehow the scum of the earth, the lowest form of life. My grandmother from my father's side used to hate me for talking about the fact that we are *Mexicanos*. But the fact is my great-grandfather Hilario was born in the Republic of Mexico on the *placer* line in the Ortiz Mountains, where my great-great-grandfather had a gold mine. He was a *Mexicano*. His relatives, my people, don't want to accept that." The idea exasperates him. "Even with Oñate there was a mix of people. That's the reality. Spaniards—quote, unquote—were the fractional minority of people who lived in New Mexico. The largest group was mestizo. Santa Cruz de la Cañada had a *casta* system. Up at the very top were the *españoles*. Then there was a group called the *criollas*. They were born in the Americas and were usually of Spanish parents. Then there were the mestizos. There were as many mestizos as there were *indios*.

"During the census, the people would come to the padre taking the rolls and say, '*Quiero ser español.*' I want to be Spanish. And he would put an *E* next to their name. I remember looking at the census records and saying, 'Wait a minute. Where did all these Spaniards come from?' Because if anything Santa Cruz was more mestizo than almost any community in New Mexico."

"But hasn't that changed? Isn't the focus now more on being New Mexican?"

"Partly, yes. We have an allegiance to *Nuevo Mexico.* Maybe it has more to do with family and culture than anything else. But that will never die. The New Mexican flag with its Zia symbol represents who we are. The other one is the imposed flag and with it came the imposed ideas."

"So much of the cultural identity in the valley seems to have been rooted in the soil," I say. "Do you feel that, too, is shifting as people take less and less of their living from it?"

"When we talk about the land," he says, speaking now as the idealist, "we need to think about future generations. My great-great-grandchild is going to use this land. That's the concept of land tenure in New Mexico. I know that Myra Ellen Jenkins, who was the state historian before I was, has written about the Italian basis and the Roman basis of land. Maybe there is some truth to it, but that's not the main factor governing our land. Basically, the message in the past was: we don't own land. That's why they didn't put up fences. That's why there were no such things as fences. There was this river, that tree, that hill over there. Those were ways to measure land. But it was owned in common. They had this common purpose. Because without common purpose you wouldn't have survived back then.

"The same system was intact with the Pueblos. Their land-use system, the way they watered, the whole *mayordomo* system was there and the Pueblos passed the system on to the Hispanos. The Pueblos had had it for many generations before the Spanish came. What the system implied is that land is to be used, not abused. If it's not used properly it should be passed into the hands of those who want to use it. That went into all land-grant contracts. It says you use this land on a trial period. We're going to give you three seasons and if nothing happens then we'll find someone else to use the land. They would, of course, consider attenuating circumstances. If the Utes attacked you fifteen times in one year then they could understand why you wouldn't want to hang out there.

"The whole concept of land tenure is not complex. Remember Reies López Tijerina?" he asks, referring to the activist who'd fought over land grants and attempted to reacquaint the Hispanic people with their roots (see pages 156–57). "He liked to talk about the smoke screen that had been put up by the entrepreneurs. And he was right. Things here are simple and clear. The life of the people is as clear to me as the sky — especially now in the fall." He smiles. "It's that clear. But there were people who said, 'Gosh, this is too clear.' We've got to do something about this. We've got to smoke-screen it. We've got to make it more complicated. People can't live this simply."

His statement outlines, in part, the problems Hispanic people have had in moving into the present century. They missed an essential step between the eighteenth and twentieth centuries. Everywhere the emphasis is different. Science is suddenly a factor in every aspect of life, even farming.

"They complicated it, and people's lives became complicated. Now, every day, I have to deal with those complex lives at this desk. I work with the displaced homemakers, the ex–drug addicts, the ex-*pintos*, and the dropouts, all the people who couldn't bridge the gap. I try to help them unravel the loose ends and tie them up. They really do have very simple lives, and somehow the system made them confusing. They come out of one system, one set of values, and find themselves faced with a system that stresses an almost opposite set of values."

"Did Tijerina remedy that?" I ask.

"Many people are down on Reies López Tijerina. They say he's from Arizona, he's really not one of us. I disagree. We didn't get our land back, but it put us on the map. It made people aware that we are human beings and we have feelings and that we actually do get educated. He's a preacher, and he did become a fanatic about affirmative action. But he helped us as people. Had he not I wouldn't have gotten a job in Denver. Yes, Reies López Tijerina helped me get one of my first big jobs. I wouldn't have had a chance in hell otherwise. I had the education and the experience for the job, but I was down at the bottom of the list. The only edge I had was that affirmative action had been created out of all the revolt. That got me in the door for an interview. And that's all I needed. They wouldn't even have interviewed me before. I got the job, as a department chairperson in history. I was twenty-four years old, really young for the job. But I went in there and sold myself."

He shoves his chair aside and sits on the desk, facing me, his hands grasping the wood top. "See, there's another message here. It is about our differences as Hispanic people, our background, our education."

"How do you mean different?"

"The Anglo establishment says if you don't know when the Magna Carta was signed then you're really dumb. I say let's look at something else. Let's take the *Recopilacion de Leyes de los Reynos de los Indios* and let's go to Harvard and see how many of their top students can come to grips with that one. They wouldn't be able to come close to pronouncing it much less figure it out."

This particular work, *The Laws of the Indians*, published in 1681, was a codification of Spanish law used, in part, to govern the establishment and regulation of colonies in the New World.

"Yes. We are different here," he emphasizes. "Tomorrow I'm going to speak at Pojoaque Junior High about the heroes and heroines of New Mexican history. One thing I will tell them is, 'Let's face it, guys, George Washington wasn't your forefather.' We need to get our priorities straight. We need to know who we are, who our ancestors and forefathers were. I was one of those kids who ran home after school and told my grandma I learned about George Washington. *'Como fera este George Washington?'* she wanted to know. Who was he? 'Why are you advertising these people? Who cares? These people don't really affect your life.' That's the difference I mean. There are interesting twists in the dual identity of the Hispano people here in the valley. Like my *tio* Juan. He died among his own people and in his own culture. He only spoke a little bit of English. Basically he was a Hispano, a *manito*."

"And you?" I probe.

"I'm not a *manito*. I mean I could be termed a *manito* in some respects, but I got educated, I speak English, I fly off to some big cities and see theater; I listen to classical music. There are some aspects of me that are *manito,* but not enough. A real *manito* is a person who grew up totally in the traditions of the New Mexican Hispano culture and learned everything in Spanish and was a very strong Catholic or *penitente* and viewed the world from the perspective of that core identity. The *manitos* are dying every day. We lose all that they had within them. They were very much unaffected by the majority society, the Anglos. They didn't fall for it. They didn't buy a TV set, or if they did they didn't watch it themselves. It was for the children. They had too many real things to do to be sitting down in front of a TV.

"My *tío* Juan's day never really ended. The guy would get into the house after dark and there was still something else to do. Then it was time to work on his tack. Indoors or outdoors the guy was always busy. My grandmothers were *manitas.* They shared with me in Spanish what their *manita* world was about and that I treasure and that I still dream about in Spanish. It's very much untranslated and uninterpreted. There are still living *manitos,* some of them in their thirties. But today they are rare. I hope there is a resurgence. I always hope for those things.

"*Manitos* are individuals who have for generations hacked out a very simple if meager life, but a very beautiful life, I think, in that it was very pure. Their integrity and honesty is the thing that amazed me so much about my grandparents, how truly honest they were. That sense of honesty, the depth of it. You never take anything for nothing. You work hard for everything you get. Most important, you follow principles and your word is more important than anything you could sign. If you say something, you follow through with it. And that is something that is, I'm sorry to say, very much gone from my own generation."

Roadside Attraction, near Velarde

The Myth of the Cultures

They say that to do injustice is, by nature, good; to suffer injustice, evil; but that the evil is greater than the good. And so when men have both done and suffered injustice and have had experience of both, not being able to avoid the one and obtain the other, they think that they had better agree among themselves to have neither; hence there arise laws and mutual covenants; and that which is ordained by law is termed by them lawful and just.

PLATO
THE REPUBLIC

I chose a place where I could live among magic and beauty, where I could touch real earth, breathe clean air, and be a part of nature not yet under the protection of the Sierra Club or held in trust by the Nature Conservancy. I wanted to be where there was harmony between people, balance between people and land.

I spent my first few months in New Mexico learning about the land. It was immediate and accessible. I was drawn to the pueblos by drums, mesmerized by the dancers. I explored villages, climbed hills, walked arroyos, and experienced a year of seasons before I began to appreciate my neighbors and how they lived.

Their lives seemed veiled in mystery. The Native Americans had been protected by their religion and by their own obstinacy. After their initial encounters with the

Spaniards, they had learned to keep their secrets; and that had helped to preserve not only their traditions but their uniqueness.

I knew the local history—a time line like Ariadne's thread that I could pursue doggedly into the past; it was an exercise in matching up names, counting centuries. However, like most history, the pages on New Mexico reduce it to a description of topography and a discussion of salient acts. I wanted to register something deeper.

From the local chamber of commerce came a catchphrase, "tri-cultural unity," words with a tantalizing ring, perfect for propaganda mailings to businesses and individuals who want assurance they aren't moving into a community of deadbeats. The chamber suggested that northern New Mexico's three cultures—Native American, Hispanic, and Anglo—exist together in absolute harmony. It was good rhetoric for slogans. But as Tony García, from San Juan Pueblo, said the year before he died: "It's pure bullshit."

The myth is not that there are three cultures. The myth, as Tony put it bluntly, is that they work together, that they ever really have—or ever will. And, as he went on to point out, why should they? Who needs it? In Tony's view, a show of unity with the conquerors certainly never had been of any real benefit to the Pueblos.

A number of people suggested that if I wanted answers I should speak with Paul Gonzáles, a San Ildefonso tribe member recently elected president of the Board of Regents of the Museum of New Mexico, the first Native American to serve in this capacity. Gonzáles, whose work in state government and tribal politics had left him with a certain savvy, had gained prestige with his election to the office, and he saw in it an opportunity to effect change; but his election had also provoked an outcry from a number of Native American artists—clear indication that there was little unity even within a single culture. Gonzáles, however, took the opposition in stride, declaring that it gave him a place to begin.

Paul and I meet in the lobby bar at the La Fonda Hotel, a place I associate with better days, when the writer Frank Waters and a few local artists were regulars in the hotel lobby, when it served as a quiet refuge from the summer heat. Now, like most of Santa Fe, it suffers under a designer facelift and the crush of too many out-of-towners from places such as Akron and Tokyo with their automatic cameras and shopping bags.

Drums, San Juan Pueblo

Paul surprises me. Over the phone, he described himself as tall—six feet three—and trim. I pictured one of those gaunt, elegant native faces with high classic cheekbones and chiseled nose, like that of the Santa Clara artist Joseph Lonewolf. Paul's features are less than angular and he carries more flesh. We sit at a small table. He orders a Bohemia. As he launches into the subject of the cultures he paints his finger through the moisture that beads the squat beer bottle.

"Last year, I was on this television show about the problems of the 'tri-cultures,' which I think was only a name dreamed up to give it some appeal. Its perspective was really only Anglo and Hispanic conflicts. I think it was only a last minute thought to include Indians—as if we might not have anything to say anyway." He flashes a smile. "The guy must've thought, Hey, wait a minute. We called this thing 'tri-cultural' but we don't have an Indian. We'd better get one." He laughs. "The guy calls me up a few days before the taping. I said—and I was sincere—'I'm glad you at least considered getting somebody to represent the Indian people.' I heard this uncomfortable silence on the phone.

"The program started with the Hispanic guy talking about how his culture in New Mexico was all bent out of shape by the Anglos who had robbed them of their heritage. I had a hard time keeping from cracking up. You know, just laughing and rolling on the floor. The Hispanic guy was a professor and he kept overintellectualizing, presenting everything at a theory level, the way you do in a classroom. The other guy, the Anglo, had been around forever, a laid-back old geezer who pretty much accepts everything. Which makes him an authority, right?

"The Hispanic guy kept on about how his culture was being exploited and what a tragedy it was. Finally, I couldn't take it any longer. I had to say: 'You know, this is all really very interesting, but we Indians view you Hispanics and Anglo guys as the same people.' I didn't do this in a mean way. I was not being hateful. I said, 'You guys think that just because you were here a hundred years before the Anglo guys it makes your heritage more important than the Anglo heritage. We Indians see you as part of the same thing.'" He shakes his head and raises his brow. "That opened up the can of worms.

"In the end they edited it so not much was really said. No one could be offended. It was just a TV newsmagazine."

Already Paul is glancing at his gold watch. He agrees to talk more and suggests we meet Sunday morning at Ojo Caliente, the hot springs north of Espanola.

On Sunday I leave Alcalde early, detour across the Lyden bridge, and stop at the base of the long wedge-shaped mesa that runs parallel to the Rio Grande. On the east face are hundreds of petroglyphs, messages the ancient inhabitants of the area etched on the dark stone—Kokopelli the flute player, snakes, the sun, animals, men represented as circles and puzzles. Recently other, newer symbols have been added, the thin crosses of the "passionists" and the initialed hearts of lovers.

I skirt the mesa and continue to Ojo Caliente, arriving an hour before Paul, and drive above the town to the proto-Tewa site of Sapawe. White clouds are beginning to build over Truchas Peak, in the Sangre de Cristos, to the southeast. It is early July, the time of year when mornings dawn clear and crisp and the midday heat draws down hard afternoon rains.

This particular site was home to the ancestors of the present-day Tewa. Evidence here and at another site, Hungpovi, near El Rito to the northwest, indicates that there were large, well-organized settlements, villages that once covered acres and housed thousands of Pueblo people; such orderly complexes reflect a harmonious and industrious lifestyle that characterizes the present-day Pueblos. Each settlement bears the outlines of walls for numerous structures, and among the ruins is a liberal sprinkling of painted and micacious shards. On two sides are traces of terracing that indicate sophisticated farming techniques; it is the work of individuals who understood the value of water conservation.

Paul is waiting when I make my way down from the ruins. His weekly visit to the baths, in the shadow of Sapawe, where some of his forebears may have lived, is almost a ritual. He comes here to relax and prepare himself for another week at the Santa Fe office where he serves as an assistant bureau chief in the Department of Human Services.

Paul find the baths cathartic in many ways. "They open the pores," he jokes, "and loosen the tongue."

The low building housing the men's spa is steamy and close. Hot water, percolated up out of the earth, pours into the pool from a rusted pipe. Warm sand shifts beneath my feet. The conversation around us is in Spanish and English, the speakers often mixing

THE RIO GRANDE BOSQUE, EL GUIQUE

the two languages in a single sentence. An old man slips into the room housing the big pool. His spidery body is crisscrossed with surgical scars like a crudely drawn map. "*Buenos dias*," he greets, scuttling over to the edge of the pool. "Hello . . ." He pulls the thermometer out of the water and holds it at arm's length, squinting to read the temperature. "*Ejole!*" he cries. "One hundred and eight! *Madre de Dios!*" His voice echoes. "Go for broke!" He plunges in, and splashes water on his face and head.

"I think I have a very interesting background," Paul says, sinking down until water laps against his chin, "partly because I have a good mixture in my family." He scoops water into his face, then clears it away with his fingers.

I ask what he means by "mixture."

"Well, my father is Tewa from San Ildefonso Pueblo. My mother's side started off in Trinidad, in the Caribbean. My grandfather and my grandmother on her side were island people. My grandfather was a brilliant student, with a formal British education, and he was accepted into college when he was thirteen. He came from a family well known in Trinidad and there were opportunities for him there, but he had no desire to pursue an academic career. He wanted to be a musician—so he moved to New York."

I find Paul's statement confusing. He has Native American blood but he is also descended from Caribbean people whose roots reach back to Europe. Nonetheless, he claims his father's race and maintains steadfastly that first and foremost he is Native American. In this he says he finds no conflict.

"My mother," he continues, his face beading with sweat, "was born in Brooklyn, raised a hard-core Dodgers fan." That makes him laugh. Like many Native Americans, Paul is passionate about baseball. "My grandfather, as he became more successful as a professional musician, moved to Los Angeles, to Hollywood, where the action was. My father spent time in California, where he met my mother."

"What was your father doing in California?"

"That was a time in the history of our illustrious nation when our leaders were trying to force Indian people to move away from the reservations," he explains. "For a long time they were mere prisons. But we must have seemed too comfortable in them. So they decided to move us out."

It was an initiative called relocation, which encouraged native people to go to the cities. It provided the incentive to go but no justification for being there. Even today, as a result of that program, there are cities with major Native American populations. Denver, Los Angeles, and Chicago are three that surprisingly have large numbers of Native American groups with no ties to those areas whatsoever. I had met many "urban Indians" in those cities and in New York, San Francisco, and Seattle. The most stirring of the images I remember were of men and women, sometimes with their babies and young children, sitting on curbs or throwing up behind garbage cans or sleeping off a drunk on a park lawn or panhandling to get money for another pint. Other more sophisticated Native Americans were given to hustling the Anglos who, lost in their own bewildering world, now sought salvation on the Red Road, which the hustlers were selling as the Indian Way.

The government's unstated objective behind relocation was to demoralize the individual and thus undermine the strength and unity of the tribes; the hope was that the tribal people would be absorbed, that they would disappear as a distinct race. The end result, they claimed, would be equality and freedom—except no Native American familiar with his people's history would believe he'd ever be accorded the same equality or freedom as the Anglo.

Paul moves to the edge of the pool and boosts himself onto one of the steps. The wet skin on his shoulders and chest glistens. "My father went to a boy's school in San Francisco. During the Second World War he joined the Navy. He never talked about the war," Paul says. "This is typical, I think, of Indian people, of their 'no ego' attitude about the world. He didn't say much about the war until years later, when I was trying to help him get a disability pension. He had an illustrious career as a navy gunner on a destroyer escort. He had a distinguished tour, with a Silver Star and a Purple Heart. But he'd been getting screwed out of his disability check for years.

"One of the most interesting things he told me had to do with traditional principles, with our native religion. He said, 'You know, all the time I was out there I kept thinking about the help I was getting from back here, from the spirit world. That's what kept me going. It made it easier for me to believe in the war and what I had to do.' "

Swimming Instructor, Espanola

"Were you surprised that it would come down to religion?"

He wipes moisture from his arms in long, slow strokes. "Not really. Religions are a dime a dozen around here. People are always trying to get us to join this church or that church, like they are afraid Indians won't find God or something. It's what the Spaniards were doing. Everybody's got this different Jesus they want us to buy, the Methodists, Baptists, Mormons. I had gone through college by then and I was trying to reconcile a lot of things in my own life. And when he said that, it brought a lot of things together for me. Anyway, the most important thing he said was this: 'When I was out there I realized something, and this is something you too must realize. I was born an Indian and I'll die an Indian. That's it. No matter what else you try to do, no matter who else you think you are, no matter what kind of life you live, the bottom line is you are an Indian.' And I think that simple statement has been a real guiding force for me."

"You must've been aware of that before," I suggest.

"It was never brought home to me in the same way. When I went through school I shuttled back and forth between Los Angeles and San Ildefonso because my dad wanted to be here and my mother liked Los Angeles. I got the best of both worlds, picking up things that affected me positively on both sides."

I sense Paul's reluctance to impart the whole story. "Didn't you ever feel that by doing this, by being both places, you might be losing your tribal identity?"

He shakes his head. "No. Many people have problems adjusting to other cultures. But a lot of good can come from taking what they have to offer. You just have to remain rooted in your traditions. I know who I am. I'm comfortable with myself. I'm proud of my mother's island blood. But I also know that the real me is the Indian part. No matter what else I do, no matter how I appear—if I wear a tux or a G-string—I am still an Indian."

We climb out of the pool and, drained and lethargic from the heat, move slowly into a large, low-ceilinged room filled with narrow beds. The attendant, a wiry man with tattooed arms, covers each of us first with a sheet and then with a coarse wool blanket, tucking it in at the chin.

"What does your Native American blood mean to you?"

"My philosophy is simple," he says. "I am as important as any other thing on the earth, any other part or piece. I am as important, but no more important, than a dog or a bird or a rock. Everything in my world has its place. And if you take away any one of those things, the whole just starts falling apart.

"The non-Indian has the tendency to think man is first and foremost important."

Paul's use of the term "non-Indian" appears to separate, in his mind at least, native people from everyone else. I ask him what he means.

"When the non-Indian views himself that way, then anything he does to satisfy himself is okay. I see it as a rationale for taking advantage of things, of people and situations."

This is a possible scenario; but can this blame for the ecological breakdown, for example, be laid at the doorstep of any single group of people? The native people are themselves users, exploiters. "Do you feel there can never be a unity between the cultures?" I ask.

"No. But the cultures won't come together until there is a unity within each culture. The contradictions have to stop." His voice trails off and I realize, hearing his heavy breathing, that the heat has put him to sleep.

The images of the petroglyphs, and the ruined dwellings at Sapawe, float briefly before me. Then I feel the attendant's touch, as he mops sweat from my face with a towel and tucks the blankets closer. For a moment I am anxious, then I, too, drift into sleep.

Earlier, Paul had labeled money an Anglo idea. Now, after sweating under the wool blankets and taking a rejuvenating shower, we venture outside into a drier heat and he picks up the theme. "I think the way a person views money counts for a lot. We talked about the idea that you are a whore if you are into just making money. I accept that. If you want money because it's going to make your life easier or give your children some advantages, then there's a logic to it."

Does he think the Native Americans' attitude toward money sets them apart from Anglos?

"Definitely. Indian people don't really have that ruthless money drive. But as outside influences get stronger, as they see money is necessary to survival, they are starting to learn. Greed can be contagious. When I notice this trait in other Indians, I think it is disgusting. But when I see it in non-Indians, I think 'Well, that's just the way they are.' " He throws back his head and laughs.

"Come on," he says, "let's go sit down. I'm drained."

We cross the yard, which is landscaped with river stones to mark the paths through rough, dry tufts of grass, and a few pieces of weathered willow-switch furniture. Paul pauses to pull two sodas from the cooler in his car and we take them to a low, shaded stone wall.

"I was on a panel about the exploitation of Santa Fe, one of those things where you had all these people getting up on their high horses and pontificating." He stands and assumes a Santa Fe voice, playing the worldly Indian, the Indian with savvy. " 'You know,' " he mimics, " 'we've got to keep Santa Fe clean. Bla-bla-bla.' They started lamenting the fact that Indians on some reservations are allowing people to put up billboards. I stopped them and said, 'Why is it that as soon as the Indians catch on to how you guys make money, you want to stop it because in the hands of the Indians it's suddenly going to spoil the earth or something. It's not like you've never seen a billboard before, but as soon as Indian people figure out how to make some money from something we saw you doing first, you start to complain.'

"Don't get me wrong," he says seriously. "I, too, think billboards are ugly, but I don't think the tribes should stop putting them up because they're ruining someone's view. The tribes are making money off them and the tribes need that money."

To the north the storm has gathered; lightning forks out of slate-colored clouds and drives at the hills. Thunder growls and dies away. "Economic independence for the tribes in this area is absolutely essential or they're just going to be absorbed by everything that is closing in around them—Anglos and Hispanics, the people with money, with political power."

He opens his soda can and takes a long drink.

I ask how his enlightened views, government job, and man-about-town style fit with his traditional ties. Aren't they in conflict?

"Maybe people expect me to be something else. I don't know. As far as my traditional background, my kiva religion, nothing comes before that. I've held jobs where I've had to tell bosses outright: 'If it comes down to me having to choose between doing something with my tribe or doing something here at work for you, I am going to choose my tribe. You have to accept that when you hire me. There are times when I have to participate in ceremonies at the pueblo—even if it means losing my job.' I have been in a couple of situations where I have lost jobs because of that." He sighs. "It's not easy." Again thunder rolls down from the hills, its voice echoing along the rocky bed of the river.

"When did you know you had to make that choice?" I ask.

"I discovered my traditional religion sometime in my young life. I can't tell you the exact day. It's something that happened, a natural phenomenon in Indian culture."

"Wasn't there a certain age when you were inducted into the kiva?" Even as I ask it, I realize my question reflects how we as Anglos want answers that conform to the same calendars that govern our lives.

"We have all these fathers and grandfathers, our elders, and they have a unique way of teaching. They say: 'Come watch me, come be with me, come see how this works, come learn about it.' There is no pressure. At some point in your life you are enlightened, ready to go on. It is like a sign. The same goes for any clan you might join. Let's say you want to be a drummer and you say, 'I've been watching this guy drum for fifteen years. I really love it and I know all the songs. I know I can do it. Will you let me drum?' The elders will say: 'Go ahead. It is obvious you want to do it.'

"That is our way. We learn by experience, rather than picking up a book, reading about how to beat a drum, and then going off to drum."

A single-engine airplane approaches from the south, flying low, banking to follow the course of the river or avoid the dark wall of clouds boiling up in the east. Paul pauses to watch it for a moment before continuing.

"The good thing about the traditional life is that I am not forced to do anything. The elders say, 'This is yours if you want it. This is what we offer you, what we give you.' I can accept it or not, to do with it whatever I want."

PUEBLO SINGERS

"And you've chosen to commit to it?" I ask.

He nods. "It begins with simple things like responding to the world around you. When I see a dead animal on the road, I feel bad. The other night I was on my front porch, it was late, and this bird came flying from somewhere and hit me. It scared the living shit out of me, but the bird had smashed into me and I thought I had hurt him. He was all right. But it brought out my concern. It touched something in me that says yes to life, that ties me to the bird and to the rest of the world. That is a reflection of my traditional upbringing."

"I know you inspire controversy outside of the pueblo," I tell him. "But what about inside the pueblo? What do your people think of you?"

"I am respected in my world but my people are uneasy about me and what I do. The elders are not sure how much they want to let me have. There is a little bit of anxiety, a little bit of apprehension. They are not sure whether I'm going to go out and tell everybody or not."

I can understand the tribe's skepticism. Paul is smooth and worldly, which might make others hesitant about him. Probably, too, his eagerness to go to bat for his people, to spend his life in government—partly, I suspect, on their behalf—makes him too visible and perhaps more than a little suspect.

"What do you do about it?" I ask.

"Work hard to make sure that they know I'm all right." He smiles. "The traditional life is full of rigors. I go through ceremonies that would cause ordinary people to collapse or give up.

"Last year, for the first time in my life, I danced in another pueblo—because I have a godchild there and I made a promise when he was born that when he decided to dance on his feast day I'd dance with him. But it was hard for me, hard to go to another pueblo and dance."

"Why? What was so difficult about going outside?"

He is too at ease in the non-Indian world, as he prefers to call it, to make me think of him as timid.

"It's about protection," he says. "The center of your universe and your energy exist in your village. I really feel that more now than I ever have. The protection and the medicine I have in my village is real strong for me. I feel very confident about that. I go to another village and I feel vulnerable to other people's power and other people's bad or good vibes."

"Is this normal for most people in your tribe?"

"Indian people are called superstitious and it is a fact. We really are. We worry about things like being away from our home village.

"Anyway," he says, picking up the story, "I was dancing at Santa Clara. It was one of the hottest days of the year and I could see that the heat was getting to the people in the crowd. They looked like they were ready to collapse. I'm not in great shape. But I danced all day long, like I was floating. And after we had been going for hours I felt stronger than I did when I started. I danced like crazy. After it was all over the war captain came up to me and said, 'Man, you sure do dance good. Thanks for coming over and helping us out.' That made me feel great. I had brought some energy to him and he had felt it.

"People don't realize that when we have a ceremony we are dancing for everyone. We dance for ourselves, for each other, for the tourists. We dance for the entire world. Even though we may be very secluded in our villages, we have a world consciousness. We think globally. We always have. We are concerned about the balance of everything.

"Indian people have been depicted as being pagan worshipers, isolationists, and not aware of world affairs. But that's wrong. All my life I have known people in my village who had an acute awareness of the outside. My grandmother used to talk about Los Alamos. She talked about the atom bomb. In the beginning, the people up there used Indians as domestics because Indian people were not considered security risks. Why they thought that is beyond me. They figured we would pass high-security scrutiny. They took Indians up there to work by the busload.

"One time at dinner my grandmother said, 'You know, those people up in Los Alamos thought we didn't know what was going on.' I asked, 'What do you mean, Grandma?' She said, 'I used to work in this professor's laboratory. I was the only one allowed in there. Not even his wife could go in.' She laughed. 'I wonder if people thought he and I were doing something together.' Then she said, 'You know, I used to pick up these little pieces of paper off the floor and there were all these funny scribbles on them. I didn't understand when I was looking at them what it was, but later on I realized what that guy was doing.' She said it in a humorous way, but there was also a note of sadness in it, which really got to me. She felt that she had been exploited, tricked into working on something she would never have approved of. Which is just typical of what we've been through in our whole involvement with the non-Indian world."

"She could look at it with humor," I suggest.

"Yes. There's a great humor in the Indian culture—even down to the most serious things. We go into the kiva and at first everything is solemn. There is always one guy, who may be a *koshare*, a clown, who right in the middle of all this solemnness does something hilarious and everyone starts laughing. You don't see that in a church or synagogue, you don't see it in the Mormon Temple. I am talking belly laughs with people actually rolling on the floor, unable to stop. It brings it all down to reality. Come on, we like to say, don't take everything so seriously.

"But," he adds, "we are serious. Our people are concerned about the world. The only input we have, our only control, is through our ceremonies. We have Indian songs that tell about things that have happened around the world, even in ancient times. One of the Zia Pueblo songs talks about the Red Sea. I mean, who here in the Pueblo culture two thousand or five thousand years ago knew about the Red Sea? Yet it is in that song. And there are other songs that mention areas we now know about and know where they are. But in the days when the songs were composed, I don't think they had that information. As the Indians become more globally aware, we start relating things from our own culture to the things we are learning. We discover that we have been talking about this or that for five hundred years—and the rest of the world is just now getting to it."

"Some people talk about universal truth—an event or idea that occurs in two or three places at the same time, without any party being aware of the existence of the other or his endeavor," I say. "It is part of a theory put forth by the physicist Max Planck."

"I'm talking about something else, too," he says. "I think that one of the big injustices shown toward the Indian culture is that people do not recognize the fact that we have been very scientific in our approach to life. People view our stories as mythology. I mean, Darwin wasn't the originator of the theory of evolution. The Indian people were. Natural evolution is the basis of all our creation stories. And they are much older than Darwin. Our elders tell us these stories the way you hear the parables. We talk about coming up from the underworld, emerging from the underworld. We have stories about the animals that helped us get to where we are today. It's not literally that we popped up from underground and were suddenly human beings. No Indian really believes that, although we preach it in the sense that if you think about evolution, you think about coming from a certain kind of underworld. Isn't the ocean the underworld? And aren't the animals that help you the animals that you have evolved from through time to make it possible to get to this point in your life?"

"Doesn't that teaching obviate the theory of the land bridge?"

"God, I hope so," he says. "It is very difficult to tell Indian people that they came from China or Japan. It's insulting. We are discovering older and older evidence that tears down the theory of the bridge and supports the Indian belief that we came from here. Why can't people just accept that? Why do all these Anglos want to tell the Indians how we came about? Indian people are very insulted by that. You rarely hear them say it in so many words. We've just held our tongues. We don't tell the Anglo how he came about; we let him have his life.

"There are all these struggles between the outside world, the Anglos and whoever else, and the world we are trying to preserve," Paul says. "We are trying to preserve it for outsiders as well. Which is a real paradox because to some people it seems like we're trying to separate ourselves from the rest of the world. But that separation is really an attempt to try and preserve the world we have. For me, the paradox in modern life is trying to deal with non-Indians and relate to what they're doing in their attempt to relate to the Indian world. Then we can try to figure out how these two worlds are ever going to survive."

Lightning strikes close by. The earth shudders, the report almost instantaneous. Paul and I run for our cars. The first few drops hit the top of my truck with a sound like popcorn popping. Lightning strikes again, the raindrops now suddenly larger and falling with such intensity that the buildings of the hot springs are reduced to hazy shadows. It is one of those summer cloudbursts that swell the rivers and turn their waters red with clay washed down from the arroyos. I sit for a moment, to wait it out and to think back on all that Paul has said. I see him as a Native American who would have an easy time of it on the outside. But he has chosen the harder path.

SANTERO, VELARDE

Santero in Espanola

One needs to see a painter in his own place to have an idea of his merit. . . . The work of the painter and the sculptor is all of a piece like the works of nature. The author is not present in it, and is not in communication with you like the writer or the orator. He offers what might be called a tangible reality, which is, however, full of mystery.

EUGÈNE DELACROIX

Ben López calls it a coyote fence. The tall, uneven line of close aspen poles surrounding his yard in Espanola sticks up like a row of wild reeds. His house, a long wall, and an unfinished building that will one day serve as his studio are faced with huge stones collected for their size, shape, and color, and laid up in a pattern reminiscent of the ponderous architecture of medieval Spain. If you look more closely, you see a design of pottery shards pressed into the gray concrete mortar, like roads crisscrossing an antique map.

Near the fence on the west side of the house, lifting up through the branches of a peach tree, its torso cast against the intense blue sky, towers a rough crucifix; it is a severe piece of work, testament to Ben's feelings about the suffering of Christ. The soft cottonwood face has begun to weather, to check and crack; the signatures of roosting birds on its shoulders and head form a white calligraphy that neither the summer rains nor the bleaching sun of August have managed to erase.

The tap of a mallet and chisel comes from under a lean-to. Ben bends over a large carving, his body moving smoothly as he brings his energy to focus on the blade of the chisel. He is stocky, with dark, curly hair and heavy features. His jeans have been washed to the point of fraying and he wears an old pair of Mexican huaraches fitted with stiff, tire-tread soles. Sensing my presence, he lifts his head. His tools, resting easily in his palms, hang like extensions of his hands. "Is it ten already? Eeee . . ." Absorbed in his work, he has lost track of the time, forgotten our appointment.

Ben talks while he finishes a small section of the carving, each blow of the mallet releasing the smell of fresh-cut wood. He is creating the altar screen for a small mountain church near Espanola, the backdrop for a Cristo he's also carving. "Look," he says, laying down his tools and blowing the curled cottonwood shavings from the open pages of a book of great religious sculpture. "I was just checking out how Michelangelo does his legs. See—with the calves and the feet together like that." He smoothes his fingers over the page, as if to caress the figure in the illustration.

Ben's workspace is typical of many local artists unable to afford elaborate studios. Agueda Martínez, the master weaver in Medinales, works in a tiny room off the kitchen in her house. Samuel Vigil in Cundiyo keeps his loom in a room with the refrigerator. Tina García makes her pots on the kitchen table and fires them in a pit in her front yard. The work is so much a part of everyday life that little effort is given to establishing a formal studio.

Ben brushes shavings from his clothes and leads the way inside. The house is small, its rooms filled with art, the work of one family laboring to honor a tradition centuries old. There are weavings by Ben's wife, Irene, as well as drawings and paintings by their children. The few works of his own that hang on the walls are pieces he has given his family as gifts. This, he says, is the only way he can keep them. His entire production goes as quickly as he completes the pieces. At the moment he is preparing for shows in Atlanta and Phoenix and a demonstration in Washington, D.C. A New York dealer has just taken a small religious statue, called a *bulto,* of San Rafael and requested more.

Detouring through the kitchen, Ben pauses to stir a batch of *salsa cruda.* He offers me a taste of it on a homemade tortilla chip. The sudden bite of raw jalapeño brings tears to my eyes.

"I'll send some home with you," he says. "But you've got to add cilantro. I couldn't get any yet today."

I pause to examine a yellowing newspaper photograph in a frame. The picture reminds Ben of a time when he was invited to lead a workshop and talk about painting at the Folk Art Museum in Santa Fe. Because the idea of a joint lecture and demonstration made him uncomfortable, he asked his kids to demonstrate the painting techniques while he talked. He grins, then tells me that that day the kids sold some of the paintings they did right off their easels.

At one end of the living room the family has created a shrine, cast in shadow. Among the objects is one of Ben's huge, carved crucifixes. It is rendered in the soulful, elongated style one encounters in El Greco's portraits. Christ's open wounds, like those on *bultos* from *moradas*, the chapels used by the *penitentes*, appear raw, tinged with blood. The hands of the Christ are big and expressive, the knuckles and joints exaggerated. This is a style Ben favors. "The hands," he says, "are the most expressive part of the body. They tell you everything."

Ben López fits easily into the tradition of northern New Mexico *santeros*. His humble origins, the hard lessons of his life, and his firm dedication to work qualify him to be included with the accomplished painters and carvers who have practiced this austere art. Like many earlier masters of the genre, such as Fray Andrés García, Pedro Antonio Fresquis, Antonio Molleno (known as the Chili Painter), José Aragon, José Rafael Aragon, Eusebio Cordova, and José Dolores López, Ben is largely self-taught, his work a continuous process of learning.

In spirit, the tradition of the northern New Mexican *santero* reaches back to the first Spaniards who ventured into the New World. Bernal Díaz del Castillo, in his *Historia verdadera de la conquista de la Nueva España*, alludes to the role religious art played in the everyday lives of the conquistadors. Cortés is said to have carried an image of Saint Peter; in *La Conquista de Mexico*, Francisco López de Gómara reports that Saint Peter, or San Pedro, and Saint James, or Santiago (often called the Moorslayer, *Matamoros*), supposedly appeared beside Cortés during one of his early battles in the New World. Bernal Díaz acknowledges this, although he admits he personally failed to see them.

WEAVER'S WIFE, CUNDIYO

WEAVER, CUNDIYO

Franciscan friars are credited with bringing the first religious imagery to the New World. During the early years of the conquest, the Order of Saint Francis established itself as a force instrumental to the colonization. In 1521 Pope Leo X issued a bull permitting two Franciscans, Juan Glapion and Juan de los Angeles, to enter Mexico. The following year, Pope Adrian VI granted shared apostolic authority to Christianize the Indians to the Franciscan Order and the Mendicants. Their authority naturally included the creation of churches and the task of supplying them with altarpieces and suitable art.

There are few reliable accounts of the extent to which religious art was brought into New Mexico. But those we do have indicate that a relatively small number of pieces were ever imported. Juan de Frias Salazar, the royal inspector for the Oñate expedition to New Mexico, made an extensive list of items being taken by the colonists and soldiers. In the inventory, compiled at the Rio Geronimo, near Santa Barbara in Mexico, we find listed various goods for barter, among them the following items:

> Six hundred and eighty metals of an alloy . . .
> Some wooden beads, painted like coral, for seven rosaries . . .
> Thirty one rosaries of glass beads . . .
> Twenty three other rosaries of the same quality . . .
> Fifty six Tlascala tassels for rosaries . . .
> Thirty one tin images, resembling an Agnus Dei . . .
> Sixteen tin medals . . .
> Some small tinsel pictures . . .

It stands to reason that many personal religious items were brought into New Mexico, though only a few warranted mention in the official list. Captain Alonso Gómez Montesinos declared that among the goods he was bringing were: "One crimson banner of damask with a picture of Christ in the center, the images of our Lady and Saint John on the sides, and on the back a picture of Saint James, the whole thing embroidered in gold.

"One taffeta banner of white, blue, yellow, and red, with two figures, the one Santa

Anna in the company of her blessed grandson and our Lady, and on the back San Diego, the whole thing embroidered in gold and silver."

Gaspar Pérez de Villagra, chronicler of the Oñate expedition, in his *Historia de la Nueva Mexico* alludes to a crucifix but makes little mention of *bultos* and paintings.

A few pieces of religious art, though never enough, were provided for in the contract between the king of Spain and the Franciscan Order, whose role it was to establish the New Mexican missions and convert the Indians. Religious imagery certainly would have been part of the baggage of the dozen or so Franciscans—priests and brothers—who joined Oñate near Santa Barbara in Mexico to make the trek north, though no one declared any to be included on the Salazar list.

In their earliest contact with Indians, the priests had discovered the efficacy of using ritual and image in what they considered their divine duty to supplant pagan worship in Mexico. W. H. Prescott writes, in his monumental *History of the Conquest of Mexico,* "It was not difficult to pass from the fasts and festivals of one religion to the fasts and festivals of the other; to transfer their homage from the fantastic idols of their creation to the beautiful forms in sculpture and in painting which decorated the Christian cathedral."

The few images that arrived by regular caravan from Santa Barbara, the territorial seat of government in Mexico, were shared throughout the New Mexican territory, a vast region that included numerous Indian missions and a scattering of parish churches erected to serve the colonists. We learn from the notes of Fray Alonzo de Benavides, written in 1624, twenty-six years after the colony was begun, that a small supply of religious art was still being brought into New Mexico from Mexico. The need was so great, however, that this meager influx of sacred objects could never satisfy it.

The images that had arrived in the territory were prized by both the churches and private citizens. The official record of those days, now held in the archives at the office of the state historian in Santa Fe, includes wills and inventories that catalog a number of altars and religious articles in the possession of colonists and their descendants.

Antonio Juan Conjuebe wrote in his will of 1764: "Item: I declare as my property a statue of St. Anthony over one-half *vara* high, and a paper *retablo.*"

Pertrona de Cárdenas, "in bed from the accident, which God so pleased to send me," dictated as a part of her will the following: "I also declare that it is my last wish that eight saints and a cross shall be divided amongst my said children."

It is revealing of the lifestyle during the early period of New Mexico that almost no mention is made of any art other than religious articles, and very few books other than Bibles. In one notable exception, Juan Frias de Salazar recorded that Juan del Caso Baraona brought five medical books to New Mexico and that Captain Alonso de Quesada declared: "Seven books, religious and nonreligious."

Not surprisingly, luxury items of any kind stood in short supply. Even regular household furnishings were scarce, because of the lack of local craftsmen and the prohibitive cost of freight.

In Spanish life, the saint was considered almost a staple. Since the days of the first colony at San Juan de los Caballeros, named after the apostle, saints have held a vital place in New Mexican cultural history. The colonists and soldiers celebrated their fiestas on saints' days, responding to any form of ritual—dance, song, and art—that reminded them of the life they had left. The padres used the crucifixes, *bultos,* and small paintings to interest the Native Americans in the church. Here, as in Mexico, they were moved more by the magic of imagery than by the words of the Mass.

To the Hispanic people of New Mexico, saints have always been important. In early times, most of them bore the names of saints. They named their towns, rivers, mountains, streams, schools, and churches after saints. The majority of art and decoration in their homes was made up of sacred objects, often no more than a crude cross, treasured images torn from an ancient book, or a picture rescued from a calendar.

The patron saint of each village, community, or church inspired its people. He or she was credited with various "miracles"—saving a life, delivering rain during a drought, or healing sickness. In addition, Santiago was often invoked for protection against hostile Indians; San Antonio was asked to help find lost objects and animals; and farmers entrusted their uncertain crops to San Isidro.

Numerous stories about the saints of northern New Mexico have long inspired the local *santeros.* Few are as colorful or dramatic as those depicting the rise into local prominence of Santo Niño de Atocha. First celebrated for his deeds in Atocha, Spain, where the Holy Child carried bread and water into the prison and measured them out with ample blessings to all the prisoners, he became known equally for his protective powers against evil and disease.

In one account the Santo Niño of Chimayo was discovered by a man and his daughter. While they were driving an ox cart out to their fields the little girl heard a *campana*, a church bell, ring from somewhere in the ground. She pleaded with her father to stop and find it. He climbed down from the cart and dug until he unearthed the bell. But beyond it he thought he saw something else. He dug deeper and found a *bulto* of Santo Niño de Atocha. The people interpreted this as a *milagro*, a miracle.

Also named Santo Niño Perdido, the patron to travelers and prisoners, the figure is reported to leave his small shrine in Santuario and walk about the countryside at night performing his good works, wearing out his shoes in the process. This has prompted people to leave shoes for his use.

Santo Niño has been stolen from Santuario a number of times, but he is always found or returned. People claim that he is protected by a special power.

The need for more images in the churches was an ongoing concern for the religious. The Franciscans, not wishing to be faulted, sought their own solutions. They were enterprising men dedicated to meeting all the problems presented by the frontier, part of which was its lack of almost any of the material things they needed to make their churches equal to those of Europe or Mexico. Circumstances and the environment turned them into architects: they were forced to construct their own churches. They introduced large-scale adobe brick making to the area, thus hastening construction time as well as increasing the possible height and stability of walls for churches and other buildings.

Because no artists traveled into the territory with the colonists, the padres themselves provided the art they needed to make their teaching more palatable. Frequently, they became the *santeros* as well as the architects of their churches. In fact, repairing and repainting old *bultos* and *retablos* and creating new ones in imitation of European and Mexican images was probably a fairly common practice among the clergy in the early days of the missions. Simple attrition from time and weather took its toll on the religious

INTERIOR, SANTUARIO DE CHIMAYO

artifacts in the New Mexican churches, but the greatest destruction came through violence. During the Pueblo Revolt of 1680, heavy damage was inflicted on the interiors of the churches and upon the religious imagery that graced their altars and walls. Of the items that lay damaged in the wake of the first revolt were a Saint Francis with his arms hacked off and numerous other artifacts found covered in excrement.

The provisional art of the New Mexican priests is targeted by Fray Francisco Atanasio Domínguez in his report upon the New Mexican missions and churches in 1776. His meticulous catalogue lists most of the imagery contained in the churches and makes careful note of those pieces he considered inferior—usually paintings, *retablos*, and *bultos* created by an enterprising priest or enthusiastic parishioner. In his description of the high altar at the Santa Cruz church, for example, he remarks rather snobbishly: "The principal niche is in the first section, and there is a large image in the round of Nuestra Señora de Rosario in it . . . Fr. García made the image, and perhaps for the shame of her being so badly made they left the varnish on her face very red."

However, Domínguez did not take a dim view of everything at Santa Cruz. "There is also a wooden bier," he writes, "painted, new, large, where is kept the image of Christ in the Sepulcher, which is very beautiful." The bier and some of the other first images by Father Andrés García were probably still largely imitative and workmanlike, but Domínguez's comments affirm that even at this early date the work of the talented New Mexican *santero* was beginning to emerge as an estimable art form.

Common to the beginnings of New Mexican religious art, a tradition into which Ben López and many of his peers fit very well, is a naive passion and dedication that, in part, make up for the lack of formal artistic training or apprenticeship to some recognized Old World master. The local *santeros* often found their teachers in imitation and improvisation. Many of these artists were even forced to make their own tools. They experimented with locally available wood that they could carve and pigments that would serve for paint. In some cases they relied upon a priest or a scriptural text to tell them how a particular saint might have looked; beyond that, they worked purely from inspiration. In so doing, they created a unique genre, an original art form, which celebrates not only their efforts but also the spirit of this isolated, strong, and resilient people.

In talking about his life, Ben is as unpretentious and direct as he is in making his art. He begins with a formal statement: "My name is José Benjamín López. My grandmother and my grandfather were my *padrinos,* my parents. In the older times almost everyone around here was named José and the middle name was what distinguished the different Josés. They used to call me Ben mostly because my dad was José too.

"I was born in Canjilon," he says and then pauses. "My grandfather and grandmother let my dad and mother build a house right next to them on their land. After my dad got sick, we moved down here to Espanola. We used to go back on the weekends to fish at Canjilon Lakes. Friends of ours close by had horses they let us ride. At least once a year, we'd go and *el jarar* my grandparents' house, you know, we'd mud plaster it. Then we'd all go rabbit hunting.

"My grandpa had three daughters—my mom, my *tia* Amelia, and my *tia* Crucita. My *tia* Cruz wasn't married yet. But Aunt Amelia had fourteen kids and my mom had eight. You can imagine what fun it was with all those kids."

"Tell me about your father."

He moves from the couch to the arm of an overstuffed chair. "I remember when my dad died," he says. "My mom came in and told us to take a drink of water, that she had something to say to us. I realized right away that she was going to tell us he was dead, because he had been in the hospital for quite a while with lung cancer.

"I was ten," he states, "the oldest one in the family. After that, my grandpa was like our dad and I grew up in the old ways."

Ben regards "the old ways" as a blessing, not a deprivation. "I remember these things about *mi abuela,* my grandma, magical things. She would have just a little bit of food warming up on top of the stove. People would come. Lots of people would show up. And just that little bit of food would be enough to feed everybody, kids and all. I say it must have been God who did it, you know, making the food go farther, because you would eat and eat and fill up. You would see that little pan with just a little bit of food filling all those plates.

"People called my grandmother a *curandera,* a healer. She used to know a lot about *remedios,* the old remedies. She healed us with them. I like those better than going to the doctor. People used to come from all over and get cures. My mom learned a lot from her but she still doesn't know as much as my grandma knew. My grandma put all those things together and they worked. I remember this one remedy. She'd start with *mula.* Then she would put in camphor, and the bone of an avocado, and the *yerba osha* — ground up, and if she could get some marijuana leaves she would put that in too. Then garlic. She would let it sit for about a month and then she would put it on bruises and achy joints like a liniment.

"She was like a calendar and a clock," he tells me. "She knew what time of the year to go to the mountains to gather the plants. She would take me with her. We would pick *osha* and *poleo,* and that wild tea. I don't know what it is called in English — spearmint maybe. It is different from *yerba buena* and it tastes different. You find it up in the mountain by the ditches. We used to get all these different weeds that are good *remedios* for the stomach or kidneys. Like *yerba de la negrita,* which helped keep you from going bald. *Yerba santa* was good for colds. *Osha* could be used for a lot of things, even to lower your blood pressure. There was another one for that too, *altamisa de la sierra.*

"When Irene started weaving, my grandma told her what to use for colors." He turns to a tapestry hanging behind him on the wall and touches it as he talks. "There's one plant, you use the root, for this light brown color. It is also good for your teeth. If you chew it, it will take care of your loose teeth. My grandfather's father used to chew it and when he died at about ninety-two or -three he still had all his teeth.

"*Mi abuela* grew a lot of *yerbas* in her yard. Things like *monstranso* and *yerba manso* and *yerba buena.* She would have that Mexican tobacco — *punche mexicano,* they call it. It has a real tiny seed. Toward the fall she would go and harvest those plants and dry the tobacco and use it to roll her own cigarettes."

He gets up and paces, catlike, the leather in his huaraches creaking.

"My mom is like my grandma in a lot of ways. She knows the old *remedios.* She just took some *yerbas* out to some Indians at Zuni. She is a remarkable woman. She has studied in Mexico and traveled all over the country. She studied things like archaeology and

HERBALIST/HEALER, TRUCHAS

Sign, Truchas

Spanish. She learned about the plants and things living with the people. My *tia* Amelia is smart like that too. She knows how to cook like my grandma. You go over there, man, she has a big old pot of potatoes and beans or whatever. You sit down and you eat comfortable. I'm never so comfortable as when I go to her house. *Ejole,* the way she makes potatoes with meat and red chile in one of those big cast-iron things. You just sit there and stuff yourself."

He rubs his stomach and smiles.

I ask him about witchcraft, about the *brujas.* He admits that they are around, at least that people talk about them still. But like most local people he is reluctant to say anything about them. There is a belief that mentioning *brujas* is *mala suerte,* bad luck. Better to keep them out of your mind. Nonetheless, both Hispanics and Pueblo people traditionally take precautions against the possibility that an enemy will try to bewitch them.

"What part did religion play in your grandparents' house?"

"Oh, man, they were real religious," he says. "Grandma was always praying the rosary, like when we would go the back way through El Rito to get to the old place in Canjilon. If we would come to a puddle or something, she would tell my grandpa, 'Okay, I'm getting out of the truck.' She would take her rosary out and begin praying, just to make sure he would get over the puddle. Once he'd made it, she would get back in the truck. 'Put that rosary away,' he'd say, like he was annoyed. 'You have me tired with that rosary.'

"I remember they'd wake us up about four-thirty in the morning to pray the rosary. Then at night they prayed again. Anybody that was there had to pray the rosary. They would close all the doors and light a candle and we couldn't go out until they were finished. After the rosary there were five or six special prayers they would say in Spanish. Then they would ask us who we wanted a prayer for. We would have to say a prayer for somebody who might be sick or needed help, even for ourselves."

"Did their influence with the rosary have an effect on your early drawings?"

"Not at first. My drawing came from school. That's what I enjoyed most in school— art. We used to have a teacher named Mrs. Boss, a real character. She used to wear like an artist's beret and apron. Her job was just to take paper around to the school. She would pass out paper and talk to the class a little bit. That was our art class. There wasn't much instruction, but it was a chance to draw. After she passed away, Mr. Montoya took over—Florencio Montoya."

He sits down again. "I liked having time to draw. I guess I was pretty good at it because for Christmas they used to have me draw a big old Santa Claus face. For Easter they'd have me draw an Easter bunny. On my own, I did pictures of hunting. I would do pictures of a man shooting a deer and stuff. Things I knew."

"Did they teach you technique?" I ask.

Ben shakes his head. "Not till later on," he says. "In junior high I got into more structured art classes, clay and papier-mâché and drawing with Mr. Montoya. Then I had an art teacher named Mrs. Amora. She cared about her students. She saw that we were poor people and she tried to guide us toward something we could turn into a career—so we could make something out of ourselves."

"Were you carving then?"

"No, that never came to me till later. But Mrs. Amora started us on sculpture. We began by putting plaster of paris on milk containers and we carved little sculptures out of them." His hands move while he speaks.

"After that we got into wood—but still not the kind of stuff I do now. Some of us were real interested and she let us work at night. For about three years we did that—three or four kids from the neighborhood. The art room was right across the tennis court."

He stands, pulls aside a curtain, and points to what is now the junior high school, the building barely visible through the uneven gaps in the coyote fence. "She just gave us the key and after dinner we'd go there and start working. A lot of nights we wouldn't come back till about twelve o'clock.

"We had a kiln for copper enameling. We would pour crushed glass on pieces of copper and fire them. The pictures were like puzzles because you can't make anything big with copper enameling or it will get a bend in it. So you have to work small and put the pieces together."

Not surprisingly, the transition to religious art was a natural process. It was suddenly there, a part of what he was doing, as if something had guided his hand.

"Some of the stuff I made in high school I sold. Like a resurrection scene of Jesus in profile. After that, the teacher asked me to make a cross for the archbishop of Santa Fe, a brand new archbishop. I don't even remember his name, an Anglo guy, a great big guy. They wanted something to go on his chair. They knew I'd had experience with enameling and asked me if I'd make it out of that. And it turned out pretty, man, real pretty. The cross was all white and I put bigger chunks of glass on the ends and they looked like jewels. I inlaid it into a mahogany board. When I gave it to him, my picture came out in the paper. My mom still has the clipping of me shaking hands with that guy."

He opens a scrapbook and leafs through it, showing me photographs of himself and his art. He stops at a page from *Enchantment,* a small publication from the local electrical cooperative. "I made that cross for the Sacred Heart Church in 1964 and they lost it. I'm probably the only one that remembers it."

Ben started seriously creating religious images after he came back from the army. It was impulsive. "I remember wanting to make a crucifix for our house. I had seen one I really liked in Santa Fe, but I knew I couldn't afford it. So I went to the *bosque* and found a piece of wood that had the **Y**, you know, and made a crucifix. I had it in the house for a long time. My old art teacher was teaching a silver-making class. He said I could take it if I'd make him a carving. So I gave him that first crucifix and I made another one for myself. But that one I gave to my brother. After that I made another one that I gave to Irene's sister. That's how I started. I did make a crucifix for us, finally, that one right there, that Russian olive one in the elongated style. We've kept it because I gave it to my daughter—so I wouldn't sell it.

"After that, people started asking me to make *santos.* I began paying attention to the art we have here. I realized it was unique. I got together with other guys who were also carving and we talked about it and tried to help each other."

I ask about his method of working. He says he calls into his mind everything he knows about the particular saint he plans to do. He thinks about it constantly, even while he is choosing the piece of wood he will carve. Those facts help determine the shape it will take. He crowds all this information into his brain and uses it as his inspiration during the time he is working on different parts of the carving. He lets it guide his fingers and his imagination.

The Cristo is one of Ben's favorite subjects. It was, after all, the impulse to have a crucifix that got him into carving after the war. "I admire Jesus so much for the kind of person he was. I like to do Jesus suffering, you know, on the cross—like that." He points to the big crucifix in the shrine. "It reminds me of everything Jesus had to go through when he lived in this world. He was a real good man but he wasn't appreciated. And I see people in the same situation today. Friends of mine. They don't seem to be getting anywhere now, but I know that later on they will get their reward—in the afterlife, when they go to heaven. I like to do Jesus to remind me of all those things."

Another figure he has a special feeling for is Nuestra Señora de Guadalupe, the Holy Virgin of this hemisphere. She is depicted with Indian features and her entire body is surrounded by a halo; usually she is shown with Juan Diego to whom she appeared in the village of Tolpetlac, Mexico, in 1531. Hers is one of the great inspirational tales for both Hispanic and Indian Catholics in the New World.

Juan Diego was on his way to Mass at a church in Tlatelolco on the outskirts of Mexico City when the voice of a woman came out of a cloud that hung over a hill. When Juan Diego approached, as the voice bade, he saw the Virgin Mary. She promised that if the bishop would build a church on that hill she would help the poor Indian people of Mexico. When the bishop heard the story he put little stock in it. The Virgin insisted that Juan Diego go again to the bishop. His interview had the same negative results; however, the bishop's interest was piqued and he demanded a sign. The Virgin promised to give Juan something the next day that would convince the bishop. But the next day Juan stayed at home, nursing his uncle who had fallen ill. The uncle grew worse and on the following morning Juan set out for the church to bring the priest to say the last rites. He attempted to avoid the hill but the Virgin met him nonetheless. She informed him that his uncle was well and said he should climb the hill and pick the roses he would see growing there. He brought them down and she placed them in his *tilma,* a kind of apron he wore, and instructed him to take them to the bishop as a sign. When Juan opened his *tilma* to show the roses to the bishop, the image of the Virgin was printed on it.

"I've seen the Guadalupe for a long time," Ben says. "Before we moved into Espanola we used to live in Guachupangue, that little community just before you get to Santa Clara. The chapel is Nuestra Señora de Guadalupe. On feast day the Indians dance and afterwards there is a procession and they carry all the saints around the chapel and then they shoot a shotgun at the old adobe wall. After the celebration, people invite you to eat, like at the Indian pueblos. Guadalupe Day is real special to me. I went to see the Basilica de Guadalupe in Mexico City and that had a real lasting impression on me. I remembered the story of the *tilma* and Juan Diego. There were so many images in the *museo*. When I do Nuestra Señora de Guadalupe, I like to think about all these things. At first it never seems like its going to be right. I keep thinking it's going to be too ugly or something, but finally it does come out.

"The Holy Family is one of my favorites, too. Our family has always been real close, you know, and I consider this a real good model to be able to follow, a real positive role model."

Now Ben remembers something he wants to tell me. "One reason I think I do this kind of artwork is because of my dad. He died when he was only thirty-five. But he always had an influence on my life. He was a very religious man. He left me a really old Spanish Bible. The first fifty pages, just about all of Genesis, are missing. But the rest of it's there. The paper's all yellow because it is so old. But every chapter is marked with my dad's own handwriting. He made marks all through it. You can tell he really used it. And he left me one crucifix, a big one, like the ones the priests wear."

"How much does living in this valley have to do with your work?"

"Everything. I think that if I didn't live here I might not do what I do. I would be a different person."

"What makes it so important?"

Ben speaks without hesitation. "The people."

"What makes them different?"

"You can see the kind of people they are by the sharing that goes on. If the people have apples they will tell you to come and pick apples—or apricots, or chile. Just this morning I came home with three bags full of food. Anywhere you go here they will tell you, 'get some apples,' 'sit down and eat.' You don't see that so much in other places. If you're fixing your car two or three people will want to help.

"And around here the earth gives us a lot. There's adobe to build houses, and vigas, and food. We have firewood. A lot of places they don't have this. We have a lot to be thankful for."

MALINCHE AND DANCERS, LOS MATACHINES DE ALCALDE

Coming into the Century

There has never been discovered in the world a land of more mines of every quality, good and bad, than in New Mexico . . . and the Spaniards who are there are the poor ones who have no means to work them and they have less enthusiasm, and are the enemies of all kinds of work . . . as long as they have a good supply of tobacco to smoke, they are very contented, and they do not want any more riches, for it seems as if they had made a vow of poverty, which is a great deal for being Spaniards, who because of greediness for silver and gold will enter Hell itself to obtain them.

PADRE JERÓNIMO DE ZÁRATE SALMERÓN

I grew up in two worlds," Arsenio Martínez tells me as he closes a window to shut out the sound of the wind, "the old world here in Alcalde and the faster world in Ranchitos."

Arsenio is working on a new house, a structure very different from the old adobe in which he has lived for the past twenty years. The new place lacks only the final flooring, wood casing, and trim, a few details. With its Thermopane windows, a second story, and a pitched roof, this house is more typical of buildings in Colorado or California than those in northern New Mexico.

The second-story window faces south along a section of irrigation ditch. A crew of men is clearing the ditch banks of brush and debris, the yearly preparation for the irrigation season. Cleaning ditches is part of the cycle of village life established centuries ago when agriculture was the mainstay. Now the crew works at a steady, measured pace, cutting and smoothing with axes and shovels, leaving the ditch behind them so chiseled and swept that the dirt has a polished shine.

"I belonged to Alcalde, because my parents were from here," Arsenio explains, settling into a chair. "But I was raised on the edge of Espanola in Ranchitos. Right away, I was removed from my roots and I was never accepted in either place because to each group of people I belonged in the other place."

"Ranchitos isn't more than four or five miles away—"

"It isn't the distance," he says, "not something you measure in miles. It's a mind-set. These guys never let me belong to either place. Later in my life when I wanted to get involved in the culture I came back to Alcalde." He nods toward the ditch crew. "The first couple of times I ever dug a ditch, I did it here. It's an old tradition and I wanted to learn about it, but it didn't take me long to find out I didn't want to know that part," he jokes.

A big man, wide across the chest and shoulders, Arsenio stands taller than most of the locals. His coarse black hair is abundant, and in his features are both the Hispanic blood and Native American blood he claims. He is outspoken and enterprising, a believer in education and progress.

"There wasn't much here for a teenager to do," he continues. "I started hanging around with a crowd of guys five to ten years older than myself. I've always done that, I guess because I learned to shuck and jive a lot younger. I had a more mature outlook.

"Guys ribbed me because I wasn't from Alcalde. Or they wanted something because my dad was in business. 'Give us this,' they'd say. 'Come on, you've got plenty. You can afford it.' They'd say it because I was younger. That turns you off after a while. But it didn't change the fact that I wanted to learn where I came from, who I was."

"How did you answer that question?"

He props his worn cowboy boots with their high stirrup heels on the window sill. "I watched my uncles," he says. "What I remember most as a child is visiting my parents' brothers and doing things with them, as a big unit. Wherever we went, down to the river to swim, or anyplace else, there were a lot of people—fifteen or twenty of us—all family.

I wanted to be just like my uncles," he states. "I happen to resemble one uncle who died. He was tough, one of the heavies in the community. He had lived in L.A. He was a spiffy dresser. And he could dance."

His forefinger traces the stitched design on one cowboy boot. His eyes flash as he looks up. "I wanted to find out what made him excel. I wanted to gain that same level of stature."

"Why?"

"I believe there are certain rites of passage. I wanted to pass through those gates and put on a cloak that would shield me. I wanted the world to see that I had accomplished something. It was a way of proving my worth in the community.

"My uncles taught me how to ride horses," he continues. "They taught me about farming, about growing chile, what was the best seed to plant, the right way to put up hay, how to garden. They taught me about being a man with balls, a man who was good for his word. I wanted to pass through the doors they had passed through. Their example brought me into this portion of my heritage."

"Once you were plugged into the culture," I ask, "what did it tell you?"

He shifts, his chair creaking. "First, you need to understand that people around here have a strange way of looking at who they are. They are confused about their history. They refuse to call themselves Mexican. They believe that if you can say you are Spanish, then you're really something. Which tells you a lot right there. They don't realize that the Spanish want nothing to do with us. Spaniards are fair-skinned, light-haired, and blue-eyed people, and we are not that. But everybody here wants to be a little better than the next guy and they think that's one way of gaining credibility. I say look at history: the Spaniards were brutal people. Fanatics."

His own genealogy is full of surprises. "I spoke to my grandfather about his family tree. It included Edmond Martínez, a half-white man. That's a little confusing, because his father was Edmond Harvey, from the Harvey Hotel family in Santa Fe. When Edmond Harvey abandoned the mother and child, he was raised in Hernandez by his aunts as a Martínez. He married a woman from here who was part Spanish and part Indian. So obviously I'm a mix of all the cultures. And for me to stand up and say 'Don't

WOODWORKER, ESPANOLA

WOODSMEN, ALCALDE

call me a Mexican' would be stupid. My wife's family is more directly tied to the Span-ish, but they don't wear that on their shoulder. They've been diluted too.

"I always say I'm a Mexican. Because I am. I am a New Mexican and if I wasn't a New Mexican I'd be an old Mexican." He chuckles. "I'm almost half Indian, Navajo and Apache. But no Indian would accept me—for being diluted, mixed. I could never be an Indian like I could never be a Mormon. I could never be a white man because I'm too much Mexican."

The wind gusts, rattling the panes, and along the river the tops of the cottonwoods, newly in leaf, begin to dance and roll. I ask how he learned about this discrepancy between his neighbors' outlooks and their attitudes about themselves.

"I learned about the valley from watching it come through the doors of my father's business. While the other kids were out doing sports and having fun I was busy learning business. I had to hold in my frustration with this because of our business. After a while, you get confused about your own emotions and why you can't express yourself the way other people do. But the customer gives you your livelihood so you don't antagonize him. Besides, if you are from a family in business, as I was, people view you differently. They think you have more money. They think you're spoiled and not in tune with your cul-ture—which," he remarks cynically, "boils down to not being in tune with the hardships."

This expression of anger and bitterness in Arsenio's voice is unexpected.

"When you are young," he explains, "you have this alienated feeling that growing up in the valley means you can't"—he struggles for words—"you can't ever be anything, that you have to go somewhere else to amount to something. You can't become anything here. You can't become really educated. You can't attend the best schools. You can't be the best artist. You settle into mediocrity. You know you're always going to be from the sticks. You just settle for that."

His description of local life as a dead-end street calls to mind a glaring headline I read in the *Rio Grande Sun* my first week in the valley. It said: MAN OUTSIDE BAR ATTACKED WITH AX. Almost every week since then the local paper has printed one bizarre story after another. A more recent headline announced, PETACA WOMAN CHARGED WITH MURDER OF FATHER. The article reported a shooting that took place in a mobile home during an argument in which the woman accused her father of killing his own father fifteen years earlier. On the same page was an article about an Espanola Valley substitute teacher who'd been "fired for packing a gun."

"Do you think the desperation you're talking about explains the fact that we are surrounded by violence?" I ask. "Do you think the frustration you see in the young people, what you said you've felt yourself, and the violence are connected?"

"The violence here goes back to the Wild West," he replies. "It's not just our people or where we live. It's simply that people out here have always had to protect their own. Only recently have we had a law enforcement agency in the valley that was worth a damn. For a long time we had two or three state cops and, I mean, what could they do? We always had to take things into our own hands.

"Then, too, it goes back to machismo. Guys say, 'How can I ever stand up in front of my friends if I let this guy walk all over me.' A lot of people feel that way. Guys here'll fight to the death to save face."

"Isn't there more to it than machismo?"

"Ultimately I think the violence is pent-up aggression from never being able to get anyplace with your life. You have to release it somewhere. There is an undercurrent of violence around here, and when it finally explodes, man, it is really bad."

I mention one of my neighbors who recently paid a visit to his estranged wife and, following a seemingly senseless dispute, shot her in the head.

"He could have just slapped her around," Arsenio says, "maybe beat her up. He didn't need to see her splattered all over the side of the house. I guess he had a statement he wanted to make and he just used her as the vehicle."

"You're a part of this culture," I say. "Have you ever felt that impulse toward violence in yourself?"

"Yes. But myself, I try to walk away from these things because I know I too am capable of making a mess of things."

"You're still talking about machismo, right?"

"Partly," he says. "But it's complicated. People here don't want you to think they're hiding behind the law. Back east and in most metropolitan areas people do hide behind the law. They think they can abuse you verbally and once it starts to become physical then they can just retreat and take you to court. They'll evict you, they'll sue you—but they won't confront you man to man. And that man-to-man thing that happens around here comes from the Wild West, in my opinion. But it can end in nothing good. It's Machiavellian; it has to end in someone's death. I guess it's not really truly Machiavellian, because you don't go in and eradicate everybody. But to save face and show everybody how they mean business these guys think it has to be really nasty and dirty, and really violent."

"Why does it have to be violent?"

"The violence comes from being pressed to make a statement and not having any other form for making it. You know, being frustrated. A sense of low self-esteem. It all boils down to one thing," he says, returning to an earlier theme, "you are from here and you are afraid you are never going to get away from here. You have to be satisfied with staying and knowing you can't make it. People don't like that. They want to be a part of what is going on; they want to succeed in someone else's eyes. They want to belong to the hip and knowing, the movers and shakers."

"What keeps them from achieving this status you say they crave?"

"Lack of effort. These guys don't want to expend the energy needed to accomplish anything. Like concentrating on your grades when you are young. Most people around here will say, 'Okay, you're getting ready to graduate from high school, it's time to go to college, so you'd better start studying.' By then, the best school you're going to get accepted by is some podunk community college that's desperate for students."

"Did this happen to you?"

"I did better than that. I was more focused. Still, I was naive. When I was growing up all I knew of the outside world was the state offices in Santa Fe and the lab at Los Alamos. Everybody here works for one of those two entities. And it's pretty hard to get an accurate cross section of American life from something that narrow.

"That's why, when I went back to learn about my culture, I studied dances that relate to our history. I danced at the University of New Mexico with the Ballet Folklórico. While everybody was out marching for La Raza and the brotherhood, I danced for the movement at all the rallies. The Brown Berets kept telling us that the Chicano movement would get us ahead. That was rhetoric. I wasn't sucked in. I tried to show something deeper, the power of our traditions. That's where I thought our strength was."

"You harbor all of this bitterness about the valley," I say. "Why don't you leave?"

"It's not the valley," he says in defense. "I love this place. It's the predicament the people are in that bothers me. We could be doing a whole lot more to bring this valley into the twentieth century. For instance, everybody around here talks tourism but no one does anything about it. We offer nothing for the tourist. Zip. I was just in Cozumel and the Mexicans down there do everything for their tourists. In Colorado, it's the same. Santa Fe's the same. Here, we expect someone to take care of us forever. We are in no rush to do anything. If they raise the price of gas on us twenty-five cents a gallon we might make a fuss for a day but we pay the extra price per gallon. In the valley, we don't commit to anything."

"Can you change that?"

"I hope I can help. Our history is unique and I always wanted to be tied into it. At one time, I thought the Matachines would be a way to do that."

The Matachines dance is a local Hispanic tradition. It was brought from Mexico into New Mexico by the early colonists. However, its history is much older than the conquest. It is an ancient dance with roots in North Africa. In the eighth century the invading Moors introduced their version of the dance into Spain; during the long occupation, it took on various Spanish elements, including some of the trappings of Christianity. The Spaniards brought the dance to Mexico in the sixteenth century, where it was influenced by the richness of Aztec culture. Events from the conquest were woven into the plot and the dance assumed new characters—Cortés, Montezuma, and Malinche. It was important to the village of Alcalde, as it was to all the Hispanic villages that had kept it alive in the centuries since the colonizing of New Mexico. One year Arsenio took over leadership of the group. He recruited fresh, young dancers, thereby revitalizing the pageant and widening community interest.

"My uncles on my father's side danced the Matachines," Arsenio goes on, speaking now with renewed enthusiasm. "My mother's brothers did it and my wife's grandmother was *mayordoma* for nearly a generation, keeping the tradition alive. When I wanted to get

MALINCHE, LOS MATACHINES, EL RANCHO

into it, to do my part, what I found was just a bunch of envious people. It was a big struggle. There are people here who, instead of working communally toward something good, will work to make things fail. That weakness permeates our history."

In his own life Arsenio tried to make up for those shortcomings. "I feel I was pretty lucky to get the Matachines. They had really fallen apart. I wanted to do something with the group, thinking I was doing a community thing and hoping everybody would get behind the religious aspect of it, and that we would all push as one. The dance, as I saw it, was basically about religion. But every time we got into the celebration, religion seemed to be put on the back burner."

Other problems presented themselves. "People wanted me to cater to them, to take them by the hand, which made it hard to instill community spirit. The Matachines had become a closed unit. That's the reason it was falling apart. No one new could gain entrance to the club. I tried to change that by training younger dancers. I wanted these kids to carry it on. I wanted to bring our culture to the world. I wanted everybody to see it. It's my opinion that if you show the world who you are you can only grow. I wanted people to see that we have something valuable tying us into times past. The oldest people I knew could talk about the oldest people they had known dancing this Matachines dance. I wanted to belong to a tradition that had been here since the first Spaniards arrived. It was a dream I had. In the end, people turned on me. I was accused of exploitation and letting the secrets out."

He shakes his head. "What a farce. I was ostracized by my own people."

"When you encountered those problems, why didn't you drop it?"

"I'm not that kind of man." His pride wells up. "I took over partly because of my kids. I wanted to tie my daughter to her culture. And I wanted to believe we can all share something. She danced the Malinche and that added something to her life. We just have to go in and learn the real meaning of what we are doing and what we stand for. For instance, why do we have the procession for Good Friday? And why are the *penitentes* a part of our life? I was never content looking at my culture from the outside. I always wanted to be a part of it."

DIRECTOR, OÑATE CENTER, HIGHWAY 68

In the Sun

mi poesia es aun un camino en la lluvia
por donde pasan ninos descalzos a la escuela
y no tengo remedio sino cuando me callo:
si me dan la guitarra canto cosas amargas.

(my poetry is a path through the rain
which barefoot children take on their way to school
and I am defeated only in silence:
if they give me a guitar, I sing of bitter things.)

PABLO NERUDA
MEMORIAL DE ISLA NEGRA

The *Rio Grande Sun* building sits on a quiet back street in Espanola, one block east of the highway to Abiquiu and Chama, just in view of the site of the proposed plaza. It is a single-story structure with half a dozen paved parking spaces in front for customers and a larger unpaved lot on the south side for employees. The entryway is devoted to shelves of office and school supplies; beyond the reception desk is an alcove framed by portable racks that display books and pamphlets about the Southwest.

At the desk a short Hispanic woman with a stiff hairdo and large-framed eyeglasses is writing up a want-ad order for a farmer who would like to sell a pen of young pigs. She holds up a finger: she'll be only a minute. From somewhere in the newsroom comes the squawk of a radio monitoring the police frequency.

His ad completed, the farmer shuffles out of the office. I tell the woman I have an appointment with the editor. She shows me to his office, promising he'll be right with me. The staff meeting, she says, is running late. Right away I notice the awards and citations received by the paper and Bob Trapp, the editor—framed certificates and brass plaques mounted on varnished wood. Their number comes as no surprise. The *Sun* is a vital force in the valley and fearless in its reporting.

The *Sun* has the look typical of local weeklies found in small towns all across America. The newsprint feels grittier than that of the big-city dailies. In general, the reporting in most weeklies tends to be insipid, the writing plodding, with photographs made from drugstore negatives. Most of these papers are chatty and inane; to fill up the space around the ads they report almost anything, right down to family reunions, church bazaars, and backyard barbecues.

The *Sun* exhibits few of these shortcomings. The Espanola Valley generates an abundance of sensational news, and the *Sun* puts it in print. A reporter who once worked in the valley before moving on to a larger paper suggested to me that with the cop killings, revenge murders, and all the senseless violence that erupts along this stretch of the Rio Grande, running a successful paper here was a cinch.

There's more to it, of course. The handling of one recent story illustrates the *Sun*'s exceptional editorial policy and its high caliber of reporting and writing. A recent execution-style shooting by Ricky Abeyta, a twenty-nine-year-old Chimayo man, left seven people dead, including a six-month-old baby and two police officers. It was the *Sun*'s kind of story. The front-page headline read: SLAUGHTER IN CHIMAYO. Under it, in a mosaic, were photographs of the seven victims and the accused killer. The facts were simple. Ignacita Sandoval had come to Daniel's Arroyo in Chimayo to move her belongings out of the mobile home she had previously shared with Abeyta. Helping Ignacita load the things into a U-Haul trailer and two pickups were her daughter Mary Ellen Sandoval (who had brought her six-month-old son, Justin), Mary Ellen's boyfriend Macario Gonzáles, her thirteen-year-old son Eloy, two sisters, Cheryl Rendon (accompanied by her three-year-old daughter and six-year-old son) and Celina Gonzáles, and Celina's friend Peter Martínez.

LA LOMA VISTA

Deputy Sheriff Jerry Martínez arrived after the shooting began. He brought a restraining order he had previously attempted to serve on Abeyta. He was shot beside his car. State patrolman Glen Huber, in Chimayo to investigate a car theft, apparently heard the shots and drove to the mobile home. He was shot in his car. Eloy Sandoval was wounded when he ran from the house. Celina Gonzáles smashed a window, grabbed three-year-old Nikki Rendon, and fled the scene. Peter Martínez and six-year-old Roland hid under a bed until the shooting had stopped.

Abeyta raced into the hills. A massive manhunt was organized by local and state police. Abeyta made his way to Albuquerque, where he turned himself in to the state police.

The *Albuquerque Journal* and the *Santa Fe New Mexican* sent out teams to cover the killings. They reported the facts and devoted some space to the story before reverting back to recycling the thin wire-service releases coming in about the impending war in the Persian Gulf. The *Sun,* whose news of that war was pretty much confined to profiles of local boys who shipped out and an assessment of the impact of the crisis on the local economy, did a first-rate job of unearthing the facts surrounding the murders and bringing the whole scenario into perspective. It presented the most sensitive account of the tragedy, exploring areas other papers left untouched. The *Sun*'s reporters gave a clear account of Abeyta's character in the eyes of his family and neighbors and opened up the question of police incompetence. More important, the story pointed up the fact—citing statistics over a yearlong period—that this kind of family-related violence is all too common in the valley.

The Abeyta story demonstrated the excellence one expects from the *Sun.* You buy the paper because you want to read it, not simply to look up movie schedules at El Pasatiempo or get a blow-by-blow description of the action at the Sun Devils' basketball games.

I hear the sounds of people starting back to work—a typewriter clacking, the copier humming. A lean man with silver hair steps into the office and introduces himself. Bob Trapp. He wears a crisp blue-and-white striped shirt and khaki pants. He has the demeanor of a newspaperman, not the clichéd big-city reporter with the crushed felt hat and the loose tie, but the more relaxed country newsman accustomed to working a different beat. Even now, when I stop to picture him, something about Bob Trapp makes me think he belongs in a green eyeshade and those celluloid cuff protectors designed to keep ink off shirtsleeves. He exhibits a newsman's work habits. While we talk, his fingers stray across the desk to pick up a pen, as if he were about to make a note.

"We started the newspaper here in 1956." He clasps his hands behind his neck and speaks in an easy, relaxed manner. His voice has a dry quality that seems to underscore his air of professional detachment. "A friend and I were looking around for a place to buy a paper. We didn't have any money. He was on a paper in Alamosa, Colorado, and I was working in Great Falls, Montana. His boss told him Espanola needed a newspaper. So we came down and looked it over. We talked to some of the businessmen. At the time, the Santa Fe *New Mexican* was putting out a little paper here called the *Espanola Valley News*. People in the valley were dissatisfied with it. They wanted a local paper of their own. We talked to some of them and"—he smiles—"borrowed a little bit of money from them. We got enough together to buy some equipment and started this thing. And it has managed to survive."

He and his partner found the support they needed. They rolled up their sleeves and went to work, and the paper took shape rapidly.

"We didn't set any guidelines or anything," he goes on, rocking back in his chair. "My partner was in advertising and I was strictly news. Our basic idea was to give the people a substantial local newspaper and make a go of it. We wouldn't play any favorites with advertisers or anybody else. We would just write the news and let the chips fall where they may. And that's what we've continued doing for the last thirty-five years."

I ask if initially he'd had any problems adjusting to life in the valley.

He turns slightly, his face in profile, and strokes his chin. "No," he says, "both of us were from southern Colorado. My friend came from Trinidad and I'm from up in the San Luis Valley. So northern New Mexico wasn't really that strange to us. It was a continuation of southern Colorado. The environment, the economy, the people were no surprise to us. If I'd have been an Easterner, there would have been some culture shock. But I went to school in La Jara, Colorado, a small town of about six or eight hundred.

Half of the people there are originally from northern New Mexico. I went to school with Spanish kids all my life, so I pretty well understand the culture."

"In those thirty-five years you must have observed a great deal of change in the culture in this valley."

"I don't think there have been a lot of changes in the culture," he says. "The Spanish families still live the way they always did. They are close. They still place family first. People here still take care of their old people. I don't think anything's changed a great deal, except economically. People have come to rely more and more on the government for their livelihood than when I first came here. And there might be less of a work ethic than there used to be. That's a normal thing, though. The more money that becomes available from the government, the more likely people are to just accept it. But basically things haven't changed much."

"What about Los Alamos? What effect has it had on life in the valley?"

"When I arrived, Los Alamos was still a closed city. But it wasn't too long after that—I'd say within the first year or so—that they opened it up. The thing it has changed most is the economics."

"How much has it helped economically?"

"A lot."

"That in itself must have brought about some cultural change."

Culture is not the word he would use. "People from here have been able to go up there, get a paycheck, and continue to live here like northern New Mexicans. Los Alamos hasn't changed their lifestyle much."

There is an opposing point of view among valley people. In the space of a few miles and an increase in altitude of about a thousand feet, people from the valley, who drive to the hill to work five days a week, make a leap from the eighteenth century to the twenty-first century. It is as if every day they enter a time machine bound for the lab and then reverse the process to drop back into the valley. They show little consciousness of what many see as the terrible potential of Los Alamos, and little memory of the destruction for which it was responsible. Bob Trapp views it practically: "Los Alamos has raised the standard of living. People have more than they did before Los Alamos, more money, more of almost everything. Now you have people from up there who live down here, participate in the community, and contribute to the life here. For the Hispanic people just the fact that those jobs are available and that they are well-paying jobs has really given the valley an economic boost. I don't know what it would be like without Los Alamos—for any of us. A short while ago I pointed out in an editorial that without the lab I'd be running a twelve-page newspaper instead of a twenty-eight-page newspaper, because the payroll wouldn't be here. We might only have one supermarket instead of three—simply because people wouldn't have the spending power. It's had a definite impact. But even though these people—sometimes both husband and wife—might work at the lab, when they come home at night they're Espanolans, Chimayoans, valley people."

Recently there has been an outcry in the national press about the dangers of Los Alamos. Staggering questions are being asked about solid waste management at the lab. How secure are the 2,400 sites? What has been the effect on the surrounding area of the radioactive fill that went into road making in the 1960s? How true are the allegations that the golf course was watered with radioactive sewage? Could the abnormally high incidence of brain tumors found in one area of the town be attributed to the presence of the lab? What risks will northern New Mexico face with the proposed Waste Isolation Pilot Project (known as WIPP), which allows the U.S. government to transport nuclear waste from the lab to a storage site near Carlsbad, New Mexico?

I had spoken to a number of people in the valley concerning the lab, questioning them about the threat of radiation and related nuclear mishaps. Mostly they were non-committal. Now I take up the point with Trapp. He shakes his head. "I don't see any prevailing consciousness about the so-called threat of the lab," he replies. "We've not had people from the outside move into the valley as much as Santa Fe has. I've followed this WIPP thing and it seems to me that the people who are really excited about it are relative newcomers to Santa Fe, maybe Taos. We don't have that element here." He dismisses it with an easy shrug.

I ask him to name the big stories the *Sun* has covered. "Big stories!" He scratches his head. "Oh, Lord! I don't like it, but our biggest story was probably Tijerina and the land-grant thing that led up to the courthouse raid in Tierra Amarilla. That and what has happened since."

He is referring to Reies López Tijerina and the Alianza Federal de Mercedes. This organization, which Tijerina founded, was dedicated largely to reclaiming land that had been granted to Hispanic people by the Mexican government and had then been swindled out of their hands in the 1800s by people, mostly Anglos, who'd preyed on their ignorance and vulnerability.

Tijerina himself was born in Texas to a sharecropper. He grew up on the move, going from farm to farm, crop to crop. As a young man he was drawn to the ministry; he attended Bible school and became a preacher in the Assembly of God Church. At one point his ministerial license was revoked. He continued, however, to preach and work among poor farm laborers and the unemployed. In New Mexico he organized the Alianza. Under his leadership the land dispute developed into a full-scale battle. On June 5, 1967, his supporters raided the courthouse in Tierra Amarilla, the seat of Rio Arriba County, and the incident hit the national news.

"It is probably the biggest ongoing story in the county," Trapp says. "And unfortunately I don't think it'll ever be resolved. It was poorly planned and carried out in a really haphazard manner, but it achieved what they wanted, which was to get attention. I think they got it by accident, but things worked out well for them. The amazing thing is no one died.

"We ran a special section on the twentieth anniversary of the raid and we had people saying, 'What in the world are you digging that up for?' They're not proud of it. A lot of people up north are embarrassed by it, upset that we came back and rehashed all this stuff. At the time, it did give a lot of attention to Tijerina's people and brought out the fact that a lot of New Mexicans didn't agree with him."

It has been said that Tijerina and his people never brought into clear focus the real issues involved in the land-grant controversy.

Trapp agrees. "Tijerina, who was the most charismatic person of all the leaders, got a lot of attention. I covered the preliminary hearings and I felt most of the people were just followers. They'd been fed this land-grant song and dance and then were just pulled blindly into it. There were probably only three people who were really aware of what was going on and what the consequences might be—Tijerina, Ike DeVargas, and Moieses Morales. They had some leadership ability. But a lot of the others were followers. They were lost and they never got a damned thing out of it."

"What about Tijerina? Did he just drop out of it?"

"Tijerina has been pretty much rejected by the land-grant movement now," Trapp replies. "I don't know if they feel he misled them or what. But he's living out in Gallina now, off by himself. He has been pretty much discarded by the others and he's into Judaism. I had a reporter interview him a while back. He agreed to an interview provided he could read it before it went in the paper and some other condition, I can't remember what it was. I said no way, no conditions. The reporter ended up going out to his house and having lunch with him, and he just spilled his guts.

"He's a fascinating personality. He could really sway people. For a while I think they thought he was going to get all this land back for them. But it didn't work."

If the single biggest story was land, Trapp believes that the most consistently interesting matter affecting the valley, the one to which he devotes the greatest number of column-inches, is local politics. The Espanola Valley and Rio Arriba County are notorious for political maneuvering and controversial elections. Valley people, especially Hispanics, are fiercely partisan and always split into camps within the parties.

"From election to election you really don't even know who's going to be friends," Trapp observes, not without amusement. "It's interesting the way the people shift sides. The politics here aren't really too different from someplace like Chicago, which is famous for its machine. Our politicians might not be as sophisticated, but they are as lively and maybe more colorful. The feature act in Rio Arriba politics is our Democratic county chairman, Emilio Naranjo."

"Why do you think politics has such a draw?" This has puzzled me for years. Every election is hotly contested. Men and women canvass the neighborhoods, stumping for their candidate, then wait near the polling places with sample ballots and last-minute instructions on casting the right vote. Sound trucks, as brash as any on the streets of Mexico, grind through the villages, blasting out the candidate's messages and repeating his promises.

POLITICS IN RIO ARRIBA COUNTY

"Politics is in these people's blood," he declares. "They enjoy it. First of all, they are enthusiastic followers, and then they become disenchanted and break away. I see that happening constantly with Emilio. He's had control of the county for thirty-five years. He has his inner group, I guess you'd call it the Democratic central committee. It's made up of a dozen people or so. You see them for a few years, then all of a sudden maybe half of them are working on the other side. You never know exactly what happened. But Emilio still keeps a core of old-timers and they never change. The other people come in and stay for maybe eight or nine years and then they are gone."

"Do you see this as a recent phenomenon, something that has developed since World War Two?"

"Not at all," he says. "In *Commerce of the Prairies*, which came out over a century ago, Gregg wrote about people here and he wasn't very kindly toward them but he did comment that they followed the *patrón* and obeyed completely no matter what he said. This went on until they became the *patrón*, and then their personality changed." He chuckles. "Again, it's an old story, the *patrón* system in action. If a guy starts getting too big, Emilio just cuts him down or chops him off and casts him aside. I can't begin to tell you how many people I've seen this happen to. One election they'll be on his ticket and the next election they're out. A guy might be elected to the state legislature for ten years and if he has a falling out with the boss then he's history. The people have elected him for ten years and he's done absolutely nothing wrong—except he had a falling out with the boss.

"It's pretty obvious some of these politicians were not elected on their merits or qualifications," he says. "It's just that old power thing. The economy has something to do with that too. Jobs. The basic things. Emilio's a good grassroots politician. He goes to funerals, gives the family twenty bucks, you know?"

I wonder whether Naranjo ever comes up against opposition, and Trapp assures me there has been plenty, but few have been smart enough or well-organized enough to damage the Naranjo machine. "One of the strongest opponents Emilio ever had," he says, "was Matt Chacon. Matt was a state senator and he died of a heart attack while he was in the senate. That's when Emilio became senator. He had the county commission appoint him. But Matt had always opposed Emilio, not on principle or anything, simply because Matt wanted to run the party."

"Did he have Emilio's kind of power?"

"Not really. Matt could always get himself elected but he couldn't get anyone else elected on his ticket. Matt was born in Vallecitos, up in the northern part of the county, and he always carried that precinct. But one election he lost the precinct and so he went back up there and had a talk with some of the precinct workers. They told him that Emilio had come up the night before the election, picked out two or three key families—the head of the family determines pretty well how the whole bunch votes—and just gave each family fifty dollars. They said to Matt, 'What could we do? For that much we can live for a month. We had no choice. We're sorry, Matt.' Matt said, 'Yes, I can understand that.' Matt wasn't upset or anything. He just said he should've been up there first with his fifty bucks."

"I hear all these stories about electioneering," I say, "fixing the ballot boxes, rigging the elections. How much is true?"

Trapp folds his hands on his desk. "The elections are interesting," he says. "But I don't think there are any more shady things going on here than in a lot of other places. Rio Arriba just has the reputation of being a tough political county. And we are the only county in the state that has had the same political boss for over thirty years. Still, all politicians do the same kind of things. They dish out the jobs. The first time Bruce King was governor, he hired some of his buddies. And when the reporters got on him about it, he said, 'Well, you don't give jobs to the people who fought you, do you?'"

"I've heard so many allegations about Naranjo's involvement in various black deeds, such as murder," I say. "How much of that is true?"

Here Trapp is careful. "I don't put much credence in the stories about his being involved in murders and all that. I've known him a long time and he doesn't strike me as that type. On the other hand, I've heard stories of him getting violent with people. There's only one story that he had a contract out on someone—with enough basis to make you think that it could be true. But I'd prefer not to discuss it. Emilio doesn't have to do those things. I think the one time that he really messed up was with Moieses Morales."

Morales had been involved in the land-grant issue with Tijerina, which had given him a degree of local visibility. He was a La Raza party candidate for sheriff; he seemed to be tugging a growing amount of hard-line support away from the Democratic party. Then he was pulled over in his car and busted for possession of marijuana.

"I'm sure Emilio planted pot in Moieses Morales's pickup and then arrested him. But as far as violence goes—I don't think so." He smiles. "If he was a violent man he would have had my place bombed a long time ago. But I've never once had a threat from him."

He recalls another story. "This happened at the state legislature. Emilio took some guy out in the hall and slapped him around because he didn't vote the way Emilio wanted him to. The person telling the story witnessed the whole thing. Otherwise, Emilio's smarter than that."

"Your paper has been relentless in its questioning of Naranjo's practices. Has that put him on the offensive?"

"Not really. He's interested in working with the paper. We have a reporter covering the county. Emilio may not like that reporter—of course he's hard to get hold of anyway—but he'll pick one reporter and hell, it might be the one who does the society or something, if he likes that reporter that's the only one he talks to. But if you can find him he'll talk to you. He doesn't spend a lot of time being county manager."

I remember my own initial encounter with Emilio Naranjo. When I first came to the valley I was intrigued by the story of this modern-day *patrón*, a holdover from the last century. Some of my neighbors were elements in Emilio's machine, and through them I made contact with him. It took weeks. Finally, I approached him with the idea of making a documentary film centered around his life. The idea appealed to his vanity. We met in his restaurant one afternoon. He spoke of his childhood, his youth, all the things he had done. He said that if we did the film he could transform one of the towns into a replica of his hometown. He seemed enthusiastic. I left my card. A few days later, his attorney, Walter Kegel, phoned me from Santa Fe and proposed a meeting to discuss this film. I met Kegel at his offices in a remodeled house on Paseo de Peralta in Santa Fe. He had a frank, crusty manner that I liked. I laid out my objectives. I wanted to film interviews with Naranjo on location throughout the valley and in Santa Fe. I also

MUSICIAN, ALCALDE

planned to talk to people who had been involved with him in various controversies. At that point I noticed Kegel's brow rise up slightly and he seemed to retreat, the intensity of his interest changing. After I had finished, he asked, rather coolly, if I absolutely needed to interview Moieses Morales and Ike DeVargas, the La Raza leaders. I explained that I had no intention of producing a one-sided portrait. I wanted an unbiased look at Naranjo, which would have to include views from people in the other camp. The next day Kegel called to say, simply, that Naranjo had no interest in the kind of film I proposed to make.

There is, however, a side to Naranjo that people have praised. "In spite of all the negative things, people tell me that he is effective in getting money for this poor county," I say to Trapp.

"People claim we are a poor county. But we're not all that bad off. For a long time, in fact, we had five million dollars in the bank. Over the years that has disappeared, but the county pretty well has what it needs. Still, we do have the reputation of being a poor county. Whether Emilio plays on this or not I don't know. But as a poor county the jobs are at a premium and he does use that. That's pretty well how he controls things."

"A smoke screen?" I say, remembering Hilario Romero's use of the term.

"You might say that, yes."

"How long's he going to keep the power?"

"Well, he's getting along in years, but there's no one that he has groomed to succeed him. It's almost as though he doesn't believe he's ever going to have to be succeeded. The younger people, those who have been attracted to his leadership, never seem to move up in the hierarchy. I don't know what it is—if he's afraid of them. The ones he keeps around him are the old-timers that have been with him for a long time. And he still brings them out and runs them for office. Take Tiny Vigil, he's been running for office as long as I've been here, just about. When Emilio steps down or retires or dies there's going to be one hell of a fight. The county won't be the same. He runs the county and it's a smooth operation. There's no problem. But there'll be some power struggles that don't occur now."

"Do you see the time coming?"

"I don't know. He had a tough time in a recent election, which was interesting because one guy who ramrodded the whole thing was a former Emilio county commissioner."

He fumbles through some papers on his desk. "Let's see—Damian Eturriaga. Damian was elected as a county commissioner as a Naranjo candidate. He resigned in the middle of the term. His story is that he became disenchanted with the way things were going. So the next election he and Jake Salazar ran, and if they had been elected the whole thing would have been turned around. They won the vote but got beat by absentee ballots. They should have known the people going into the courthouse to get the absentee ballots weren't their friends. People set up a howl. But those were legal votes and they were outmaneuvered. It's hard to get ahead of Emilio in an election. He's just got things too well thought out. He's been doing it for thirty-five years, and his father did it before him."

Of all the political contests, the most irritating to Trapp are the school board elections. Here the damage cuts deep—it is the children of the area who suffer. "As long as I've been here," he begins, "the school board has been very political. The bad thing I see is that you have a school board election and the people who get out and work for the different candidates don't seem to care about improving the schools or helping the kids. They are there to win an election and to hell with the consequences. They choose sides and decide who they are going to support and they go out and work for that person. Winning is the important thing, not what might happen to the educational system."

"Did this influence the way you educated your kids? Did you send them to private schools?"

"I had no problem bringing my kids up in the Espanola Valley. I brought three up here. We've got problems with the schools but I don't see where Espanola's problems are any different from anyone else's. We've got drugs, but everyone's got drugs. We haven't gotten into gangs so much. The guys from Chimayo might fight the guys from Alcalde. But that's only because they are from Chimayo and these other guys are from Alcalde. I don't see where it's a difficult environment. I feel the family is what determines how a kid is going to turn out, not necessarily the city or the environment. I think the family is the root of the development of the individual."

"Aside from politics, where do the big school problems lie?"

Trapp finds it almost impossible to talk about the school system without discussing politics. "The principals of the schools have been in the system for twenty or thirty years, and I have known of teachers who tried to bring in new ideas—open-classroom concepts, things like that—but the principal made it so tough on them they had to stop or get out of the system. People who try to make changes just aren't well accepted. Part of the problem too is that the young people go away to college and get a teaching certificate and come back to Espanola and teach and try not to make waves and then retire. New people coming in are not encouraged. If they need a math teacher desperately they might hire someone from somewhere else, but it doesn't happen much."

Many people tell tales of corruption and unfair practices in the school board. One man, who asked me not to mention his name, had a contract school-bus route. In order to work it, he had bought a bus, and his wife had taken a job to help him keep up the payments. When it came time to renew the contract, which he had been assured would happen, he was cut out in favor of a relative of one of the school board members. He still had the bus and would be forced to take a significant loss when he sold it.

"It goes back to politics," Trapp maintains. "So many teachers and school employees will give you information, but they say, 'Don't use my name, don't tell them where you heard this or I'll lose my job.'

"So some guy who is a janitor at the school doesn't want to lose his job and he'll do what he's told and keep his mouth shut. Jobs aren't that numerous around here. I think the board gets too involved in the janitors' jobs and things like that rather than seeing that the kids are educated. It has always been that way. All politics. But nobody will talk—except off the record."

Such fears are not confined to the school system. They extend to almost every employee in the county. "Look at other papers," Trapp says. "In the *Taos News* they've got a full page of letters to the editor. Not here. Most of the letters we get are from people who refuse to sign, or they ask that their names be left out. If you ask them why, they tell you it's because they'll lose their job or they'll have their windows broken. It's fear."

I mention a recent development in which the state board of education came to Espanola and seized the purse strings of the local school board's finances. "You have been relentless in your pressure on the school board to clean up its act. Is this part of the payback?"

"The state should have done that a year ago," Trapp states, skirting the question. "They didn't. It's the same old thing. We ran a story in the Thursday morning paper, which hits the street Wednesday night, quoting a school board member saying that the state was going to take control. We had talked to the state superintendent and he kept saying they were going to do it on such and such a date. We would call him on that date and he would say he was going to be out of town on that day and he wanted to be here when they did it, so they were going to do it on such and such date. We just kept getting stalled, so finally we ran the story and at eight o'clock on Thursday morning the phone rang and it was the state board of education saying, 'We understand you ran a story saying we were taking over the schools. Where can I get a copy of it?' It turns out that until the story came out they weren't going to move. But once we'd run our story they had to do something. And that's when they came in."

"From what I understand, it had to do not only with money that seemed to be missing and in somebody's pocket or somebody's relative's pocket, but it also had to do with some pretty stupid money-handling practices."

"In a business," Trapp says, "you withhold taxes and social security from the employees. In my case I go to the bank every two weeks and I deposit that money and they hold it for two weeks and make money off it and then send it to the government. Anyone in the school system should know that you send that money to the government on time. The schools had been making those payments late. The feds frown on that. They penalize you if you don't make it on time. The IRS fined the school board forty-six thousand dollars for late payment. You could hire two teachers for that."

This reflects a certain arrogance that characterizes local politics. I had attended a few school board meetings. Many of the members struck me as having difficulty expressing themselves in either English or Spanish. Instead of significant intelligent debate, there was a show of the kind of petty backbiting and fumbling stupidity that clogs up the democratic process.

"Where do you think the fault lies?" I ask.

"When I came here in 1956, we had a superintendent of schools, with the principal of the elementary as a sort of assistant superintendent, and there was one clerk, a payroll clerk, and that was the entire administration. Now we've got a whole building full of people up there. I don't know how many cars they drive, how many offices they have, and they can't even get their damned money to the government on time. The bureaucracy is incredible. Part of the problem is the sheer number of people. They're falling all over each other. And every damn school board member's got someone he wants to give a job to. It all goes back to the idea that you win the race and then take advantage of the position and forget about improving the schools."

Trapp would like to see more change in the school board, but because the corruption runs so deep any real turnaround will be slow. Still, he is determined to keep trying. He believes his newspaper can provide a forum. He uses the *Rio Grande Sun* in every way he can to improve the life in the valley. He has, as he said earlier, let the chips fall where they may.

BROTHERS, ESPANOLA

Brother of Light

The idea of the whip as a means of grace is one of the oldest in the history of nations. Herodotus tells us that the ancient Egyptians flogged themselves in honor of Isis. The boys of Sparta were whipped before the altar of Artemis Orthia. In the Roman Lupercalia devout citizens esteemed it a felicity to be struck by the leathern thongs of the Luperci. And by the beginning of the fifth century the Christian church came to recognize the virtues of the lash for offending monks — a remedy to whose efficacy several provincial councils testified. About the end of the eleventh century, Cardinal Peter Damian preached and practiced self-whipping as a penance, and inspired a considerable following. About 1210, St. Anthony of Padua founded the first fraternity for regular and public self-practice with the rod as a religious ceremony.

CHARLES F. LUMMIS

I'll call him Horacio Martínez. He speaks of himself as *un viejo,* an old one. He is eighty. One can read the years in his face, wizened features creased and honed by the mountain winds and hardened by the sun. Seasons of reaching down to the earth have left his body bent and stiff. Once he possessed the sinewy strength and grace of a horseman; now his body is frail, his left hip and leg bound up by rheumatism. But he remembers the earlier times, when he had energy and passion, when he possessed the youthful fire and the macho that lie at the core of his heritage. Pausing to remember those days, his lips draw into a thin smile.

Horacio has lived his whole life at the edge of the Espanola Valley. He was the first-born of eleven children. Helped by his father and three brothers, he built a house within sight of his parents' place. He formed the adobes, mixing straw with the dirt; he turned the blocks in the sun to hasten their curing; then he laid them up as the thick walls of his house. He cut the bucks that support the adobe above the doors and windows. He peeled bark from aspen to make the vigas and *latias* that support the dirt roof. His eight children had grown up in these close rooms.

Looking around the small house, I ask where they'd all slept—ten people.

"We managed," he says. "People don't need so much space. Sometimes they do better with less."

He invites me to sit. We are in his kitchen, a room added on to the original structure. The furniture is old, the majority of it handmade. Some pieces, such as the *trastero*, the old cabinet, its finish aged to a fine patina, and the table with hand-carved legs, once belonged to his mother. At some point an electric range was installed in one corner of the room near the sink. But it never displaced the old wood *fogón.* Horacio hovers close to its warped firebox and at intervals rises to feed a couple of piñon sticks through one round lid in the top. Pushed to the back, a pot of beans simmers, giving off the pungent smells of epazote and garlic. Above the stove hangs a calendar, its color reproduction depicting Jesus with a bleeding heart, almost five years out of date; I presume that it marks the year his wife died. Suspended from a large nail driven into the plaster above the table is a crucifix with a dried palm leaf wedged behind it. Two corner shelves hold dime store ceramics, souvenirs printed with the names DENVER and MEXICO.

Across the room is a small table covered with a white lace cloth. It is a kind of shrine. On it are a cluster of saints, two old ones, a hand-carved Guadalupe and a San José, and three of plaster. Hung on the Guadalupe is the rosary that belonged to his mother, a fine chain with dark beads and a gold cross.

When I ask about his education he tells me that sometimes it seemed they were still living under foreign rule. At one point, speaking Spanish in the schools had been discouraged. Then, in fact, it had been strictly forbidden and any talk about the old traditions had been unwise.

"I remember practicing English," he says. "I knew I had to sound like them—like you Anglos—if I wanted to get anyplace. It would have helped more to change my name. People did, you know. I could've become Horace Martin and maybe things would have been better for me. But it wouldn't have seemed right."

Horacio Martínez taught school, worked for the county highway department, and did day labor in Los Alamos during the years the lab was being built. Through it all, he retained his land. He farmed in the early morning hours and in the evenings until dark. He worked the same soil his father and his grandfather had plowed and planted, small fields that slope gently down to the river, now almost bone-dry in winter. He grew chile and corn and squash and a few garden vegetables. Periodically during the year he butchered a steer, two pigs, a sheep, and a goat. In the days when his eyes were sharper and the animals were more plentiful he had hunted deer and rabbits.

He can remember when there were not enough priests, not enough, at least, to visit all the Hispanic villages. "There are still villages without priests," he says. "It was worse in my grandfather's day. Then, the priests stayed mostly at the missions for the Indians. Oh, they might come once a month for a Mass in our little churches. But not much more."

The shortage of priests gave rise to *los hermanos*, the brothers, the *cofradía*, known as the *penitentes*. The brotherhood took on parish work neglected by the priests. They did not try to displace them—some things they could do, others they could not do. They conducted services; they visited the sick and dying; they buried the dead. But they could neither administer sacraments nor say Mass.

He runs his finger along the bridge of his thin nose and speaks with hesitation, calculating just how much he is going to tell me.

Before we began our talks he confessed that he was not certain why he had agreed to tell me about *La Hermandad de Nuestro Padre Jesús Nazareño*, except that at one time he had considered writing about his experience. He was quick to point out that he had no desire to reveal anything he had been entrusted to keep secret; he would not— because it was forbidden. But somehow his life had slipped away faster than he'd ever

BACKYARD SHRINE,
RANCHITOS

Jesús Nazareño, Truchas

imagined it could. Suddenly he discovered he was old and knew he would never write the book.

He pauses, spreads his thin, leathery hands, and scans them, each one veined like the underside of a leaf.

La Hermandad de Nuestro Padre Jesús Nazareño, the *penitentes,* has been a tradition in his family. For at least three and perhaps even four generations, his ancestors have gone into the *morada* (the little chapel *penitentes* use for their rites) and devoted their lives to the *pasión,* as faithfully as if they'd received a calling from Rome.

Where had the *penitentes* come from?

"Some people have said the brotherhood originated in Spain at the beginning of the last century. I know only that it has always been a part of my life." As it had been part of the life of his father and his father's father and even the father of his father's father, extending back at least to a time before the United States took over the territory. He assumes that someone brought it from Spain. Wasn't that obvious? In the early days almost all things came from Spain; the Franciscans themselves might have brought it. It might have arrived with a renegade priest. Theirs was a harsh order. No matter who was responsible for introducing it into New Mexico and no matter when it had arrived, it had come originally from God. Of that much he feels certain. Isn't it proof enough, he insists, that it came when it was needed?

Any attempt to date the emergence of the *penitentes* in Southwestern history is difficult. Historians use two reliable sources to put the brotherhood into perspective. The first is the exacting report of Fray Francisco Atanasio Domínguez of 1776. In it there is no mention of the brotherhood, though Fray Domínguez does remark on the existence of other, less important organizations. And the second source is the report in 1833 by Bishop José Antonio Laureano de Zubiria. In the portion of his letter concerning the brotherhood in Santa Cruz de la Cañada, Bishop Laureano de Zubiria makes his disapproval very clear:

> *. . . proibo eses hermandades de penitencia o mas bien de carnicería que ha ido tomando cresimiento al abrigo de una tolerancia indebida. Cada Parroco o Ministro*

*en todo el distrito de su administración cuidara de que no quede ninguna de estas her-
mandades, y que no halla en parte ringuna Recogida o guarda de estos grandes
maderos, y otros instrumentos de mortificasión conque algunos medio matan los
cuerpos tal bez al tpo. mismo qe. no hasen caso de sus almas, dejandolas estar años
enteros en la culpa.*

(. . . I prohibit these brotherhoods of penance, or rather, of carnage, which have grown in the shelter of an unlawful tolerance. Each priest or minister shall take care that none of these brotherhoods remains in any district under his administration and that nowhere is a storehouse for those large crosses and other instruments of mortification with which some half murder their bodies, at the same time forgetting their souls, which they leave for whole years in sin.)

Curiously, after his stern castigation, the bishop goes on to condone penitence in moderation; it is as if the presence of the brotherhood and its obvious power might have appealed to him had it not been on the fringes of the church. Using these two reports as a guide, contemporary historians have arbitrarily chosen the year 1797 as the date of its emergence, allowing the *penitentes* 150 years as a renegade group before the brotherhood was formally recognized by the Catholic Church in 1947. Previous misconceptions about *La Hermandad de Nuestro Padre Jesús Nazareño* and many of its practices can be traced in part to the sensational writings of the journalist Charles F. Lummis and to an old book by Alex M. Darley entitled *The Passionists of the Southwest.* These works dwell on flagellation and pain and tend to gloss over the deeper and more serious devotion these men feel for their brotherhood and for its purpose.

"In the beginning," Horacio says, describing his experiences, "when you are learning the first mysteries and becoming a Brother of Blood, when you are going through the scarification, the lashes, and feeling how it seals you to the others, to your brothers, that feeling is like nothing you ever felt before. You forget your body and think only of your soul and the glory of God."

He had imagined those first moments since childhood. One morning, after they had made certain all the men were in the fields, he and a friend crept along the road to the *morada* and peeked in the window. Excitement caused his heart to pound. The darkness inside chilled him to the bone. He was convinced that God had chosen to protect the interior of the *morada* from his prying eyes. This only intensified the mystery.

He might have asked his father about the *morada*, but his father would have said nothing; he might even have sent him out to chop wood to allow him time to consider his impertinence. As a boy, he observed the processions of Semana Santa, Holy Week. "I never remember not being a part of the processions," he says. "I walked beside my mother, my *tías*, my sisters. They would help with the *santos*. During certain years, my sisters were Veronicas. They paraded along before the *santos*, carrying the Virgin, the Dolorosa; they wore the cloth with the image of Christ's face. On Tinieblas, on the night of Good Friday, I remember *La Carreta de Muerte*, the Death Cart, creaking on its wooden wheels and bringing Doña Sebastiana with her bow and arrow to the little church. I remember the praying and singing and the candles going out one by one, until there was darkness and the wooden *matraca* began to grind and send shivers along your spine and the chains rattled. Slowly the candles were lighted again. And they did the whole thing again."

He takes a sip of coffee from the chipped enamel cup he keeps warm on the edge of the stove. "There was never a question whether I would join the *cofradía*," he says, holding the cup in both hands. "It was only *when* I would be invited to join."

That question did not need asking. There came a year when he would feel something strange and look up to find his father watching him — in the fields, in the corral with the livestock, at the supper table. "I had grown. I was no longer a boy. I knew that. I was trying to become a man, although my body wasn't always willing to cooperate. It was then that my father took me to the river. We had our fishing poles and after we had baited the hooks and cast out our lines and watched them settle he talked to me about the life of a man — about how we were to be with women. It was hard for him to find the words and sweat popped out on his forehead." He chuckles. "I only appreciated how difficult it was for him years later when I began taking my own sons to the river.

"In the same year as our talk, in the winter, *los hermanos* came to me." He closes his eyes, as if to see it more clearly. "It was evening. My mother and sisters left the room. The brothers talked about God. They asked questions I could barely answer—my mouth was so dry. When they finally left, the sound of their voices seemed to be still echoing in the empty room. I realized I was shivering."

His voice falters. "In the spring, on Martes Santo, I went to the *morada* as a *novicio*. My godfather tied a blindfold around my eyes and helped me along the road to the *morada*. We stopped at the door. I was carrying the lights [candles] for an offering. I was afraid to move, afraid the hammering of my heart might be heard inside. I knocked at the door, so timid at first that there was almost no sound, then I knocked harder.

"A voice came: '*Quien toca en la puerta de esta morada?*' [Who knocks at the door of this *morada*?] Fear gripped me. My godfather nudged me with his elbow. I used the words I'd been instructed to say, that this was not the door to the *morada* but the door to his conscience.

"It is like yesterday," he says, shaking his head and staring into space. "The questions kept coming out of the dark. I replied that San Pedro would open the gate and wash me with his holy light, in the name of blessed Maria, with the seal of Jesus.

"The voice demanded: '*Quien en esta casa da luz?*' [Who gives light in this house?]

"'*Mi padre Jesús—*' [My father Jesus—]

"'*Quien la llena de alegría?*' [Who fills it with happiness?]

"'*Mi madre María—*' [My mother Mary—]

"'*Quien la conserva en la fe?*' [Who keeps it in the faith?]

"'*Mi hermano José.*' [My brother Joseph.]"

Horacio stops talking. The fire crackles in the stove. He makes a sudden move, as if to rouse himself out of a dream, and his chair creaks. He glances at the tape machine, the tape turning slowly in the tiny cassette. He seems surprised for a moment that I am present. A pickup passes on the road. "I heard the door," he says. "You know, how it sounds when the lock slides. I was taken inside. I seem to remember candles, though it may have been dark. Now, as I think about it, I seem to remember also the *pitero* blowing his flute." He frowns, his face brightening in spite of it, then goes on. "I was taken to a small room. I was told to undress and given the *calzones*, the pair of white pants I was to wear." He smiles, relishing this memory. "I sometimes think I remember wind during all this, wind blowing outside the *morada*. But like the candles and the flute it might be only a trick my mind is playing with me."

His eyes twinkle. "It wouldn't be the first.

"*El hermano mayor* asked if God had called me to serve our *padre Jesús* in holy penance and virtue and would I enter with *alma, vida, y corazón*—with soul, life, and heart.

" 'Yes,' I said, 'in the name of the Lord.'

" 'Do you embrace this congregation?'

" 'Yes, if I have offended or scandalized any here I ask forgiveness in the name of the Lord.'

"Then he asked if they would accept me. I trembled as I waited. The silence seemed to stretch on and on. Then the voices came in unison: 'We accept him and respect him in the name of Our Lord.'

"*El hermano mayor* held up a large crucifix—"

He looks up at the cross on the wall. There is a long silence interrupted only by the crackling of the fire and the sound of a lowrider passing outside, the hard bass on its boom-box speakers growing gradually fainter.

He continues: "*El hermano mayor* asked me to confess and to give my intentions.

"I said, 'Oh lord, I have sinned, have mercy on my soul.'

"He questioned my belief in the holy church. He asked if I believed in the Trinity and that God was one and all-powerful.

"I said I believed.

" 'Do you believe he suffered death on the cross, just as you see before you, to save us?'

"I said I did.

" 'Do you wish to receive the cross?'

"I said I did.

"He gave me the cross. The moment I felt its weight in my hands I was filled with joy—and fear. I kissed it and I also knelt and kissed the dirt floor of the *morada*. Even while my lips were still touching the earth, *la tierra*, I heard the brothers begin to recite '*El Verdadero Jesús*.'

MORADA

El verdadero Jesús
Nos libre de todo mal
Vanandonos con su luz
Diciendo por la Senal
Tambien de la Santa Cruz;
los demonios bengatibos
nos procuran perturbar
y asi con grandes motibos
la cruz nos ade librar
y de nuestros enemigos
me Valgo del Redentor,
en su sirbicio me ofresco
Diciendo, con todo amor
Libranos Señor Dios nuestro
Por interceson del Verbo,
y la que es del hijo madre
asi mismo me corijo.
Diciendo el nombre del Padre
Tambien el nombre del Hijo —
Mi Vista al Cielo lebanto —
Con ferbor y en el alto voz
Soltare mi triste llanto
pues que ofendo a mi Dios
Como al Espiritu Santo —
Siempre mi percinaré
Con la Santisima Cruz
a Dios me encomendare
pues que digo amen Jesús
junto con María y José.

"On my feet again, I felt the hands of the *picador,* who is the one chosen to make the cuts, massaging my back. His fingers and thumbs reached deep into the muscles, soothing and softening. And he took from a wooden box one of the sharp *pedernales,* and cut the *sello,* the seal of obligation, into my back. I hardly felt the strokes as he sliced through the skin along the sides of my spine and then across my upper back, but I was aware of something warm, the flowing of my own blood on my skin. It felt like joy, like the release of my spirit from some sad place into happiness." He clears his throat. "That is how I remember it."

After a long pause, he proceeds again. "I asked for the *disciplina,* the whip, and he struck me three times on each side. That was to remind me of the three meditations of the Holy Passion. Then I could feel the wounds. I asked for a reminder of the five wounds of Christ. The *disciplina* bit at my wounds. I asked to know the Seven Last Words, the Ten Commandments, and the Forty Days and Forty Nights.

"The pain was great, but I knew it was only a token for the pain Jesus had endured for me. I lost count of the lashes, but I did not fall. I remember smiling as I felt the cool *romerillo* tea, which is made from the silver sage plant, being bathed over my wounds."

He stands and feeds another piece of piñon into the fire. "That was the beginning," he says quietly.

I know from his tone that he will tell me no more.

My brief glimpses into the activities of the *penitentes* have been special. When we moved into Alcalde, I had no idea the brotherhood existed in the town. I assumed in fact that the *penitentes* had been mostly lost in nineteenth-century history and certainly never imagined they could be any closer than Truchas, the village overlooking the valley on the east.

Our house sits just east of the Capilla de San Antonio, the old parish church the brothers use in conjunction with their *morada,* which stands almost half a mile to the south, to stage the annual Easter season processions. The first year, the appearance of the crosses in front of the house was puzzling. I discovered them on my morning walk to

FIESTA PROCESSION, ALCALDE

the post office, small white crosses made of wood, no more than a foot high, bearing roman numerals, and stuck in the dirt at the side of the road, dividing the distance between the church on the Alcalde plaza and the *morada* into just more than a dozen stops. The processions began the next day, or perhaps the day after. At first there were only a few men. Then, as the week wore on, they grew in size.

Many of my neighbors were among the marchers, gathered to honor one of their timeless traditions. There was in each procession a complex play of symbolism, which changed from day to day. Various *bultos* were carried back and forth between the church and the *morada*. I recall a huge image of Christ wearing a blindfold, then the same figure under a red shroud. The Veronica, one of the village girls, a delicate child in black, displayed the apron upon which were sketched the miraculous images.

Tinieblas, the celebration on the night of Good Friday, recalled stereotyped accounts of the *penitentes* that I had heard or read. I waited in the dark on my front porch. I heard the sounds of the *pito*, the wooden flute, and the mournful creaking of the wooden-wheeled Death Cart and caught sight of the swinging lanterns in the distance. The men, alone now, their faces shining in the yellow lantern light, sang and drew Doña Sebastiana and her companion in the cart slowly to, and then away from, the church.

I'd been told the activities that culminated the week included a ritual reenactment of the crucifixion, taken to the point of pain in its symbolism. Throughout there was singing, the sounds of the plaintive and powerful *alabados*, the *penitente* songs, filling the village.

Years later, with my son Devon, I witnessed the Tinieblas service. Inside the church lighted only by candles, brothers prayed and sang. The candles were snuffed one by one, gradually plunging the little church into darkness. Chains banged on the floor and the *pito* shrieked. My son clutched my arm. Finally a match flared and the candles were slowly lighted and the prayers resumed.

The processions and the services were natural forms of expression, of a people tradition-bound to remember not only the suffering of Christ but also the efforts of their own ancestors to keep his memory alive. To live this ritual, to observe it as a fact of everyday life, is a rare blessing.

HOG BUTCHERING, ALCALDE

Down from the Mountains

They defended what their ancestors had forged with their own hands, the last traces of an exquisite culture, far off in the wilderness, at the last boundaries of the most impenetrable mountains in the world.

PABLO NERUDA

There came a time," Philip Trujillo begins, "when I asked my mother, 'Where did I come from?'

"She said: 'Your father bought you. He was out trading with the people in Mora and he bought you from a farmer up there and hauled you home in a gunnysack.'

" 'No—'

" 'Yes. It is true. When I first touched you, I thought you were a little pig.'

"I got mad and ran and told my father. He had a good laugh about that. Then he leaned down and said. 'Eh, *mi hijo,* don't you believe her. You came from God, like all my other children.' "

Philip Trujillo is a small, slender man with closely barbered gray hair. He wears a shortsleeve summer shirt and a baseball cap advertising a New Mexico team. We have met at his niece's house in Lower San Pedro, once among Espanola's small satellite settlements but now within the city limits. His niece herds her kids into the TV room and closes the door so we can talk in peace. In the background, the sound of *Mr. Rogers' Neighborhood* is punctuated by occasional outbursts of crying or laughing from the kids.

CHIMAYO TRADING POST, ESPANOLA

Philip removes his cap and sets it carefully on a stack of magazines on the table near his elbow. He is shy and reserved; his fingers tremble slightly.

I ask him to recall the influence his parents had on his early years in the valley. He tells me first about his father, summing up the man's life in two sentences. "My father was Nicholas Trujillo. He was born, reared, and lived his life in Chimayo—except for the few times that he went to work up in Colorado, building the railroads."

I nudge him on, asking him to name one thing he remembers best about his father.

"He was a workaholic," he replies, his comment not a negative one, coming instead with admiration and love. "He worked hard and he expected us all to do our share. Partly it was from necessity and partly from temperament. That generation didn't have enough daylight. They had to use the night. If they went to the mountain for a load of wood, they'd get up at midnight and start off so they would arrive where they were going to cut the wood by daylight."

Hard work had been the code of the valley since the colonization. "They had to work in order to survive. We had only a small farm there in Chimayo," he says. "We grew primarily chile but a few other crops too, like *cebollas,* 'onions' in English, and some fruit. Things we needed to eat."

Philip recounts his family's difficult times in a village little changed in over fifty years. The family farms, now as then, stretch along the Santa Cruz River at the foot of the Sangre de Cristos. Agribusiness, as it is known in other parts of the country, in which huge corporation-owned farms serve as convenient tax write-offs when they fail to make money, will never hit Chimayo. Today, farms like that of Philip's family are still owned by the same families who established them. Apple, cherry, and apricot orchards thrive, and Chimayo chile continues to be the major cash crop, prized by devotees for its flavor and subtle hotness.

The name Chimayo comes from the Indian term *tsi' mayo,* which in Tewa means "stone that chips well"—presumably the stone from which the early tribespeople fashioned arrowheads. Besides its chile, and, in the years before prohibition, its wine grapes, Chimayo is world-renowned for El Santuario, its healing church.

Bernardo Abeyta, a devout man of Potrero and a member of *los hermanos,* the *peni-*

tentes, is credited with establishing the church. One year during Holy Week he went into the hills surrounding this tiny community just south of Chimayo, to do penance and visit all the holy places. Not far from the Santa Cruz River, he was startled to see a shaft of bright light issuing from a hole. He approached the hole and unearthed a crucifix representing Our Lord of Esquipulas. He showed it to his neighbors, who were as moved as he was. They formed a solemn procession, carried the crucifix downriver to Santa Cruz, and presented it to the priest, who placed it in a niche in the main altar of the great church there. The next morning, however, the crucifix was gone. It was later found in the hole in which Abeyta had first seen it. Three times this event repeated itself. The people were convinced that a higher power meant the crucifix to remain in Potrero. So Bernardo Abeyta built a small chapel on that sacred spot. That church has become known as El Santuario and continues to exist as a miracle in the lives of the faithful of Chimayo.

I ask Philip how it was possible to earn a living off such small farms.

"It was always a struggle. My father used to load whatever produce we had grown and take it up to the higher villages, like Penasco, Mora, and Chacon. He would be gone about a week, peddling it to those people."

The practice was as old as these outlying settlements. Farmers traded with one another, with their neighbors, and they traveled to villages where their surplus was a needed commodity. They bartered with Indians in order to obtain different goods. Over the years they adopted many Indian farming techniques as well as local Indian cuisine, which many claim, mistakenly, is of Spanish origin.

"Everyone had to do something," Philip declares. "I didn't get out of it just because I was the youngest. We had a couple of dairy cows and my job was to take care of those cows. When my father took the family to work the chile in our fields I was left in charge of the cows. I'd tag along, walking the cows up to the pastures and then watching them. I didn't have to do fieldwork, but I took care of the cows and milked them. My father saw to that."

"Would you describe him as strict?"

"My father was a strict disciplinarian." When he makes this declaration, Philip's tone

Small Chapel, Chimayo

of voice suggests that he might have tested his father more than once. "In our neighborhood," he explains, "we had this bunch of older kids who were always getting into trouble. One time they cut the ears off a little mule that belonged to one of our neighbors. That man was sure I'd been with the gang and he told my father so. I argued that I hadn't been with them. But my father got a rope and he locked the door to the barn and he started beating me up. 'Why?' I cried. 'Why are you doing this?' And he said, 'You know why.' He gave me a pretty good whipping and I took it, but I was sore at him for taking that man's word against mine. I had never seen that mule until after its ears had been cut."

Philip remembers other incidents involving himself and his father. "I have never been able to hold on to a pocket knife. I always lose them. I borrowed my father's knife once and lost it and I got a beating over that, too."

"Was the whip the only kind of discipline he used?"

"My father always used the whip. I guess he thought it worked best. I got so many beatings that my mother used to say to him: 'Just don't hit Felipe in the head because it will make a little *tontito* out of him.' So I got most of it on my buttocks and my back. He wouldn't touch my head. He didn't want me to be a little dummy."

Philip's father had another side. He was adamant about having his children go to school. He would sacrifice almost everything to give them a chance to learn. Nicholas Trujillo recognized the value of education and its power to improve a person's life and heighten his sense of self-worth.

In rural New Mexico, the Catholic Church controlled the people from the time of the conquest. Centuries after the colonization began, other churches, attempting to gain a toehold in hostile territory, used education—the building and operating of schools in isolated communities where there was little opportunity for formal learning—as a means of luring people away from the priests. A number of those schools survive today, including the McCurdy School in Santa Cruz and the John Hyson School in Chimayo.

"The Presbyterian missionaries came in," Philip explains. "Not only them, but the Seventh Day Adventists and others, too. People wouldn't have anything to do with them because they were afraid of excommunication. The Presbyterians set up a little

Sunday school on the plaza in Chimayo and tried to convince someone to sell them enough property for a day school. Nobody wanted to do it because the priest had said the missionary teachers were devil women." Philip takes up his cap and turns it absently in his hands as he talks. "My father had no quarrel with the church but he was a man who could not have cared less what anybody thought about him or what he did. He believed that the only way out of all this mess was for his family to get educated in the ways of Anglos. That was more important than what the priest might think of him, so he sold the missionaries the piece of property on which the Presbyterian Mission School now stands. My dad made sure that all his children went to that school. It was a sacrifice. In those days, everything was barter. There was very little hard money. He traded produce. He did work. All of his kids made it through that little school and his girls were some of the first to go to the Allison James School, the high school in Santa Fe."

"Did the teachers pressure him to convert?"

"There was a missionary," Philip recalls, "a Miss Ellsworth, the principal teacher at the mission school in Chimayo, and my father used to go and plow her garden with his horses to pay our tuition. One day, she invited him to stop working and have a cold drink of water. They were sitting on a bench on the porch and she started mentioning religion. She wanted my father to think about becoming a Presbyterian. My father said, 'I have a religion already. What I want is an education for these children of mine.' "

"And he remained a Catholic?" I ask.

"Yes."

"Was it only your father who was interested in your education?"

"No—my mother, too. She never stopped talking about it. She kept saying, 'If you go to school and learn something then nobody can take it away from you. They might take your land away and they might take your clothes but what is up here' "—he taps his head—" 'nobody can touch.' "

Nicholas Trujillo did not live to see his dream fulfilled. He died in 1929; Philip was eight years old. But he had instilled in his children the desire to pursue an education and the will to fight for it.

Teacher/Herbalist, Espanola

After more than sixty years, Philip is still so sensitive about his father's death that his voice falters when he talks about it. "I remember my father was sick a lot. It turned out that he had cancer in the stomach. It took a year of sickness for him to die, but he kept on trying to run the farm. The day he died he got out of bed while we were having breakfast and he and my mother decided who was going to go work the fields and who was going to stay with him. Two of my sisters stayed. The rest of us went to the fields. About midmorning my youngest sister came riding up on horseback to tell my mother she'd better go home, that he was real sick. So my mother started walking home."

Later on, Philip's mother told him what happened that day. She'd seen his uncle, her brother-in-law, approaching with the bad news, a dark figure on a horse. She tried to be strong but when her brother-in-law informed her of her husband's death, her legs buckled and she fell to the ground. It was only with his help that she could get to her feet again.

"This uncle came and told us to go home too," Philip remembers. "My brother hitched the horses to the wagon and we started down the road. About a mile before we got to the house we noticed that some of the chile sacks had come untied and we'd left a string of chiles behind us."

The teachings of Philip's father, the unrelenting work ethic governing his life and all their lives, persisted even at the time of his death. Philip and one of his sisters were told to climb down from the wagon and pick up the chiles.

"When we got to the house, everybody was crying." Philip's voice fails. He clears his throat. "I started looking for my father, but I couldn't find him." Again he pauses. "He was so thin that he didn't make any—what do you call a *bulto?*—bump on the bed. I finally picked up the sheet and there he was. He had wasted away that much."

Most of Philip's brothers and sisters were at school in Santa Fe or Albuquerque, and those not in school were married. Naturally, they came home to help with the harvest, but of the eight children Philip was the only one living with his mother. "My work went on," he says. "I had to separate these two cows from the others, bring them in, and milk them. Then I delivered a quart of milk to the minister. He paid me a dime each day. That was our total cash income, three dollars a month."

The farm was difficult for Philip and his mother. Aside from the fields at home, in which they grew chile and other crops to can and sell, there was a large plot in Truchas that produced hay to feed the horses that pulled their wagon and farm equipment.

"All that land had to be worked," he says. Without the husband and father, the farmwork was suddenly more difficult. "The following year, my uncles, who also had land in Truchas, met my mother and my sister and they plowed the land in one day. The next year my brother, who was in school in Albuquerque, was allowed by Mr. Donaldson to come for two weeks and do the planting. I was only ten years old but I went to help. He let me handle one plow while he worked the other. The plow was so heavy it would knock me down and he'd go around me with his plow."

Shortly afterward, Philip's mother recognized the futility of maintaining the Truchas place. She could not do the work; either she had to ask her oldest son to take time away from school or she had to let someone else handle the farm. Refusing to jeopardize her son's education, she found another farmer to work the place on shares.

I ask Philip to describe his mother.

He smiles and shifts a little in his chair; then his smile fades and he grows silent again. From the other room I hear the *Sesame Street* song. One of the kids crows. The silence becomes uncomfortable and Philip clears his throat. "I hate to quote Richard Nixon," he says, "but my mother was an angel."

He laughs uneasily, his hand straying toward a small end table to straighten a couple of magazines. He turns to the window, casting about to call into his mind the image of his mother. "She was an incredible person," he declares at last. "No one can remember that she ever raised her voice or hit them. She was gentle." Then he adds, "But she was strong. She worked from sunup to sundown. She was very persuasive. She set an example. I think the character of my sisters shows the kind of person she was: she guided them."

"And you, as well?"

"She was always there for me," he says. "If I had to get up at midnight to go bring hay down from Truchas, she would fix breakfast while I hitched the horses, and when I came back with the hay she would have food ready then, too."

He remembers the hours and hours she toiled. In those days there were few modern conveniences. Everything had to be done by hand. "I wish we'd had an automatic washer. She boiled the sheets and other clothes to disinfect them. Now you have Clorox. You pour it in the machine, set the dial, and go away. But she had to be there—working.

"She used to make her own soap." He shakes his head sadly. "I wish she hadn't. Because you have to put lye in it. I don't know how she kept from going blind from it. But to her, cleanliness was a virtue. Things had to be clean at any cost. She was just as strict about honesty. She used to tell us that if we saw even a straight pin on the floor in somebody else's house we were to leave it there, that it was not ours.

"One thing I remember is how after my father's death she prayed with me and I learned the creed and then the rosaries from her in Spanish. She would say them to me in the dark after we went to bed. That is probably the best thing she ever did for me because I came to appreciate what life really is."

Philip remained at home with his mother until he started having trouble at school. "There was a lot of mischief at the school in Chimayo," he says. "Other guys were really doing it but I was getting blamed too. Those guys were older and supposed to be three years ahead of me in school but they'd been held back. They were big guys, bullies, and that made it bad. My married sister kept saying, 'Philip, don't associate with those guys.' But there was nobody else to associate with. Still, I didn't want to be characterized like they were. They'd fool around with girls and bother the teacher, stuff like that. Just making trouble." He looks up. "I'm not saying I was an angel or anything. But in the heat of all the trouble I told my mother, 'I cannot stay here anymore because I don't want to be blamed for things I didn't do.' "

That same year Philip's older sister's husband found work in Albuquerque. The family decided that Philip should go along. The move would extract him from a potentially bad situation and allow him to attend a better school. And when the brother-in-law's employer transferred him from Albuquerque to Anton Chico—in Guadalupe County—Philip went with them.

"I had a great teacher at Anton Chico," he recalls. "J. J. Clancy was his name. He noticed that I was a little advanced and he said, 'I think you can pass the eighth grade examinations.' I was only in the seventh grade then, but he arranged for the exams and I passed two grades in one year. From there, I went to high school in Santa Fe and stayed until I got my certificate."

For Philip, this was a milestone. "My brother had graduated from New Mexico State and I said to myself, I'm going to graduate from there too. So I found some guys in Las Cruces that were trying to do the same thing, and we moved in together. I got a job as a janitor in the music building for twenty-five cents an hour. I had to put in one hundred hours to get twenty-five dollars."

Carrying a full course load while working began to affect his grades. He scheduled a conference with the dean of students. "I told him I was having a tough time trying to work and study and do my cooking, too. He said, 'Why don't you take two meals a day at the school dining room?' We figured it out. Food would cost eighteen dollars a month, I had to pay five dollars for rent, and that left me only two dollars a month spending money, less than ten cents a day. But I survived."

Lack of money was only one difficulty. A worse problem was racial discrimination. He mentions that racial problems have existed in New Mexico because the Anglo minority discriminates against the other races. I ask him to recall an incident.

"There are bigots, you know," he says, shifting to the edge of his chair. "I had this one Anglo professor, I don't remember his name, but I remember he didn't like the Spanish kids. I was up with the best students, doing the same quality of work, coming up with the same answers. They got the A's and I got a B. I had to learn to live with that, but I didn't learn to like it," he says.

"I tried to avoid that guy," he says, his tone telling me how much he dislikes the memory, "but somehow he kept finding a way into my life. I was taking a course with the dean of the college of agriculture, and he died a couple of weeks before school was out. They assigned the course to that other professor. I had an A. I knew it and so did everyone else in the class. I remember the day that professor walked in to take over the class, a gringo sitting in back of me whispered to another gringo, 'Man, Trujillo's A sure went to hell fast.' I got a B. I didn't dare say anything because he could've given me an F. I just took it with a grain of salt."

"Why did you enroll in the school of agriculture? I'd have thought you'd want to get completely away from your past."

"I love farming," he says. But there is something else. "My overall objective was to come back and help my neighbors."

In his statement is a sentiment I keep hearing. The people here are not simply from New Mexico, they are from northern New Mexico. It is an important distinction to them. They are from a pueblo or the valley. They have a loyalty to their roots. "I wanted to help the Hispanic people here. If I could show them a better way to farm I might be able to improve their quality of life, and if I could do this and make their existence easier, it would give me real satisfaction. Through my own experiments, for example, I thought I might develop a chile plant that would excel in this area."

Philip's plans had to be shelved during World War II. He trained for aircraft maintenance and spent much of the war in the Aleutian Islands. When the war was over he continued his schooling, this time at the University of Maryland, concentrating his studies on crop improvement and crop breeding. "One of the most important courses I pursued there, one that really gave me what I needed for the work I later did here, was devoted to the area of probability in the scientific realm."

I ask him to elaborate.

"You take a hypothesis and you formulate a theory. Then you execute your experiments by randomizing the repetitions to see if there are certain elements in your theory that come through. My project was to work with two strains of corn that I wanted to mate at separate times. I went through several treatments, trying to enhance one while I retarded the other one. Then I recorded the data and presented the results in a thesis. It was exactly the kind of procedure I would need to use in developing a new strain of chile."

When he graduated, there were no employment openings in northern New Mexico. He took a job in the Federal Housing Administration office in Albuquerque and kept looking. Finally he heard of an interesting position.

"There was a lady named Mrs. Bartlett, a world traveler and a collector of art who owned a large piece of land in Alcalde. She had gone to the Museum of New Mexico with a proposition, that if they allowed her to have a part of the museum to house her collections she would give them the Alcalde property or any income from that property. Four state senators from this area created a bill that paid the museum a certain amount of money for the land. New Mexico State University came up with the idea of a research farm.

"I got the job of running that farm, which was exactly what I wanted to be doing. At first my ambition was to be a county agricultural agent. In that job you have all this information to transfer to the farmers, but the farmers resist taking it. You can't blame them. Anytime someone from the outside insisted they were going to help us, our people always got a raw deal. I didn't want to beg the farmers to let me help them, so I tried to work it so they'd come to me. The gates were always open."

He laughs, remembering a story he used to tell every field day, when local farmers were invited to an open house at the farm in Alcalde. "There was this little guy in school named Johnny, and his teacher noticed he was always scratching. She said, 'Johnny, why are you always scratching yourself?' Johnny replied, 'Because I'm the one who knows where it itches.'

"That's what I'd tell the farmers. You have the problem, you know where it itches. You have to come tell me so I can try and solve it for you."

Philip has another field-day anecdote. "There was this moron entrepreneur who heard a lot of money could be made growing turkeys. So he ordered seven hundred turkeys and went into business. He plowed a field and planted the turkeys feetfirst, and they all died. He figured he had made a mistake. So he called the hatchery and they sent another seven hundred young turkeys and he planted those headfirst. They all died, too. This is not working, he thought, and he decided to consult an agricultural expert. The expert listened to what had happened, thought a minute, and then said, 'You know, I think we'd better check the soil.'"

Philip is an expert with special qualifications. He is a local; he went away and returned with a solid education. During his years at the Alcalde research farm he listened to the farmers when they came to him and decided how he could best help them, beyond just handing out practical advice aimed at addressing their immediate problems. One issue that plagued local farmers was finding crops that could mature in a short growing season. For hundreds of years they had simply taken their chances and been forced to watch too many crops fail.

"Chile is our best crop around here because it is not perishable. The people know how to grow it, they trade it and sell it. So it made sense to exploit chile on a more commercial level.

"One strain of chile that I developed, Espanola One, which matures in a short season, is still in existence," he tells me. In his voice I detect a note of pride. "This doesn't happen in a year or two. It was a continuous process of experimentation that took about twenty-five years. Red chile is our most commercially viable crop. So my goal was to develop a variety that could ripen and be processed for red chile.

"We put in a weather station to monitor daily temperatures and measure the precipitation. We averaged it all out to determine the length of the growing season and we found we had 150 days in the Espanola Valley, compared to 226 days in Las Cruces, where previously most of the experimentation had been done. Which meant the crops that would ripen down there wouldn't ripen up here—even in the best year.

"I took a variety that had been developed on the Richardson Farm in Las Cruces. I selected plants and pods that ripened the earliest. Then, by selective breeding, I gradually developed Espanola One, with a maturity time short enough to match the climate in the valley. It changed the chile business up here."

"Were you able to get the farmers to respond to what you were doing?"

"Eventually, yes. It took time to develop those confidences, but the people began coming around. I started the annual field day up here so farmers could see I was there to help them. And we got along well."

His program offered a solution to the problem the university had in reaching the Hispanic population, the majority in the area. But that was apparently lost on the state officials who mete out jobs, often for political reasons. "All of that has changed now since I retired. Last month, I went to the field day. There are no Chicanos on the staff anymore, no Hispanics. You need that to keep the people's trust. At this last field day I attended, there were probably a hundred and fifty people. Among them I could count only four or five Hispanics. When I was there, it was just the opposite."

El Abuelo, Los Matachines, El Rancho

El Abuelo

And all that is good you must fight to keep with hearts
as devoted as those of your fathers who fought to gain it.

T. S. ELIOT

Rudy Herrera is a self-made folk historian who works out of a cold north room at Rancho de las Golondrinas. The Ranch of the Swallows, as its name translates into English, is a small "living museum" located in the hills of Cerrillos a few miles southwest of Santa Fe. During the early eighteenth century the raw land for the ranch was purchased by Miguel Vega y Coca. Then in the mid-1930s the Curtin-Paloheimo family bought the place; after working it for almost two decades they turned its adobe buildings, fields, and pastures into a living museum dedicated to preserving Hispanic rural traditions.

Rudy Herrera's passion for folk history brought him to Las Golondrinas after he retired from his job at Los Alamos. His particular interests are expressed by the objects in his "office"—a few choice pieces of antique furniture, an assortment of old tools he is restoring.

Rudy is a dynamo. Short and solidly built, he has a wrestler's powerful arms and low center of gravity. His face bristles with a thick growth of salt-and-pepper whiskers. As he talks he appears to be constantly in motion, rocking back in his chair, gesticulating and forming words with his hands, picking them out of the air with his fingers.

"I was born in El Rancho, New Mexico, at my grandmother's house, right across from the little church there. It was during the depression. But New Mexico really wasn't suffering that much. We didn't know the difference. We'd always been in a depression. We still are." He rears back in his chair, making its rusted wheels squawk, and laughs.

The phone rings. Rudy's hand shoots out, grabs the receiver, and disconnects the cord. "Hold my calls." He smiles.

Humor plays an important part in Rudy's life. In the community of El Rancho, at the edge of the Espanola Valley, he acts as one of the *abuelos*, or grandfathers, in the local Matachines troupe. His role, which casts him as a clown, also has its serious side, involving ritual and discipline. It is his obligation as *abuelo* to help parents of the village keep their kids in line.

Like many Hispanics, he begins explaining his background by automatically reaching into the past at least two generations.

"My family were farmers," he says, "which is one reason why I'm here at Las Golondrinas. My grandfather, Donacialo Gonzáles, made his living by farming—when he wasn't playing politics. He was probate judge in Santa Fe, then a magistrate judge. During the time he was serving one of his judgeships in Santa Fe, the family lived at the La Fonda Hotel, and later at what is now Sena Plaza."

The Santa Fe he describes is different from the city of today—smaller, remote, a vital trading center but little else.

"Some president came to Santa Fe," he says, continuing to unravel the thread of his life. "I forget which one. Spanish people never paid much attention because those guys were all Anglos, you know, and we were sort of prisoners in their country." He grins. "My grandmother took my mother, who must have been around seven or eight years old, down to the main plaza to see the president. Mom got lost in the crowd, never found her mother, and couldn't find her way back home. She wandered the streets of Santa Fe and wound up on Upper Canyon Road, where she spent the night at some people's house.

"The next morning two girls who lived in this house were outside on the porch, goofing around, combing my mother's hair with a broom and giggling—and Manuel Lujan Senior, the father of Senator Lujan, now secretary of the interior, who used to read meters in Santa Fe, drove by in his buggy. He saw my mother and said, 'Aren't you

Aguilla's little girl?' My mother said, 'Yes, I'm Salina.' And he said, 'Well, your mother is looking all over town for you. Why don't you hop in the buggy and I'll take you home.' That's what life was like in those days."

Rudy pauses to drink from his coffee mug, holding it with both hands. He takes pride in his life, his heritage. He loves to talk about the past and recounts the stories in his repertoire with a folksy zest.

"My grandfather Gonzáles was also a farmer," he says. "Barranca Mesa in Los Alamos belonged to him and his two brothers. They had about two hundred acres up there, where they dry-farmed. Manuel Lujan Senior was their neighbor. He owned Horse Mesa, out where the stables and the baseball field are."

"Was Gonzáles the grandfather who taught you farming?"

"No," he says. "All the farming techniques I am bringing to Los Golondrinas I learned from my grandfather on my dad's side. I grew up constantly sticking my nose into Grandpa Herrera's business. I watched to see how he plowed, when he harrowed, what he planted, the way he irrigated. I was always asking questions. Oh, he'd get real cross at me. He would be hammering on something and I'd stick my head in there to see what he was doing and he'd yell at me. But all my knowledge of farming with horses and hand planting came from him. I learned to pick the best animals to keep for breeding, and the ones you should geld or castrate. Later, I think it was even his instruction that led me to work in Los Alamos."

"With a family attachment to Los Alamos that predates even the lab, do you ever feel bitter about the developments up there?"

"Oh, yes," he says, with a sudden note of sadness. "There's a lot of heartbreak there. My mother has tremendous memories of going up to Los Alamos before the lab took it over. While Grandpa farmed his wheat and beans, Grandma stayed in El Rancho and tended the chile crops and melons and so forth. She traded whatever she harvested for shoes and school clothes for the kids. Grandpa would raise the beans in Los Alamos and take them down to the Bond Store—later it was Bond and Willard—who were the big merchant princes in Espanola, and he would make payments on his wagon and other more expensive implements. Almost everybody in the valley was running a charge account at the Bond place or at the old San Juan Mercantile Company, and of course they were being robbed by these so-called 'pillars' of the community. In fact, I get real mad when I think about those guys. They were our worst crooks. Once they got you under their thumb you could never get out."

"Let's go back to Los Alamos. What are your first memories?"

"I remember my mother's stories. Everything had to be brought in by wagon because the roads onto Barranca Mesa were so steep nobody could get motor vehicles up there. It was a whole day's journey by wagon from El Rancho to Los Alamos. All the girls in the family would go up to hoe the beans. Grandma would give the kids a nickel, and on the way they'd stop at the little store right there at the bridge over Otowi Crossing. Remember that place from Frank Waters's book?"

Frank Waters's *The Woman at Otowi Crossing* is a novel on the topic of the life of Helen Chalmers and the development of the bomb at Los Alamos. In Waters's narration the woman who lives at the crossing and operates the store becomes a sensitive link between the worlds of the Los Alamos scientists, their exotic experiment, and the Indians and the Hispanics of the valley. Today there is another Anglo woman living in the house at Otowi Bridge. Pamela Philip, a minister, chose it for its solitude. She, too, stays in touch with the cultures.

Rudy continues: "The kids would buy hard candy and suck on it all the way to the farm. Then they would stay up there and work for weeks before they came home. My mother tells me that she would see the faint little lights down in the valley, like lanterns, and she would be so lonely for her mother she would start to cry."

"What about you? Do you remember how things were when the big changes were happening at Los Alamos?"

"I grew up with Los Alamos," Rudy replies. "I saw the place right from the beginning. In fact, it dominated my life for a long time. Starting in 1943 or '44, my dad went to work on the hill, making fifty cents an hour, which was a very high wage for labor around here. Naturally, with that kind of money available, the men left their little farms down in the valley to the wives and kids and started building Los Alamos. It was the most money they had ever seen.

WOMAN AT OTOWI BRIDGE

"I remember when my mom and I went up to visit my dad and my uncles. I had to have a pass to go through the gate. My uncle took us to the old homestead, my grandfather's place, and my mama broke down in tears when she saw our little log cabin that had been taken over by the government."

"What do you mean 'taken over'?"

"The government appropriated it under the War Act. During the war, the government had the power to take large sections of land, anything they needed. The government did pay some people. The politicians got paid."

"But not the farmers?"

He smiles, but there is a bitterness in it. "Nothing has changed, right? Manuel Lujan Senior got paid. Big ranch owners like the Dot people and the Grants got paid. Some of the other homesteaders got fifty cents an acre—you know, something minimal. Others, like my grandfather and his brothers, never got a cent. That stuff kind of sticks in your craw."

"Were people given any explanation?"

"Not that I know of—except that the land was needed." He shrugs. "Maybe the government thought they could lump us in with the Indians. They'd been ripping them off since the beginning."

He pauses, his tone softer. "But by the same token, I guess you've got to be realistic. I'd still be a bean farmer if it hadn't been for Los Alamos. My dad wouldn't have been able to earn fifty cents an hour and later a dollar, making it possible for me to stay in school. It was a trade-off. I hate to think that our property was just nabbed like that. Because of Los Alamos we are prosperous in our area, even in comparison with the rest of the country. But I still wake up a lot of times early in the morning—I don't know why it happens in the early part of the morning—with memories of the years I worked at Los Alamos."

"What was your life like prior to going up there to work? Did you feel trapped here?"

"Trapped? Not really," he says, sitting back in his chair and crossing his legs. "During my high school years I worked at various jobs. I took care of a thousand laying hens for the Freedman family. Morning and evening, I would feed them all, gather and grade the eggs, and get them ready for Mr. Freedman to take to market. I worked with my uncle Eloy on his trucks. After that I got into the high-paying job of service-station work." Again he flashes a smile. "I pumped gas the last two years of high school at a little cut-rate station. That gave me sixty bucks a week, which was very good for a high school kid those days. I bought my own car and clothes and had plenty left over for spending money."

"And from there you went on to Los Alamos—"

"I went to work up there in 1958. I hired on as an apprentice insulator and asbestos worker. Barranca Mesa was still undeveloped, unspoiled. There were only a couple of houses up there."

Rudy admits to being a romantic. "I used to go out and sit in my grandfather's old property and remember my mother's stories about the way they did things in the old days. Working on the hill took me away from the culture and my way of life," he laments. "Even then, I knew that. As a matter of fact, I didn't speak Spanish for a few years, because everybody was speaking English. I think that's the reason I used to go out to the old homestead—even though at the time I didn't understand really why I was doing it."

Looking at Rudy today, one has difficulty associating him with the high-tech world of Los Alamos. Most of our visits together have taken place in rustic settings. At his home, he is surrounded by animals. He and his second wife, Gayle, a teacher in Pojoaque, keep horses, burros, cows, goats, pigs, dogs, cats, chickens, geese, and turkeys. He has collected old machinery, fixed up rattletrap trucks, and brought home various other antiques that line the lane from the Nambe road to his house.

Los Alamos offered the best opportunity to work in the area, with money and a promise of security, but Rudy had other ideas. "No matter how good my work was, I always wanted a college education. I got married in 1959 and we started having kids, and by the time I finished my apprenticeship in 1962 I had four kids and another one on the way. College in New Mexico was impossible, just too damned expensive with kids. Through my family, I heard that California had free education. We drove to California and found that all you needed down there was supplies. Using my uncle's address, I applied at Pasadena City College. I began attending classes at PCC and Long Beach State and finally got my teaching degree from UCLA. Ironically, I didn't like teaching. So I opened an auto repair shop and went into business."

"Other people have told me they went away and found themselves in an alien environment, enslaved to a job. Was that the case with you?"

"The hard part was being there," he says. "All the time I was living in California I was homesick. I missed my people terribly. I missed the things we did, the folk dances— Matachines, Comanches. I missed the baptisms and family things. I missed the mountains, the Sangre de Cristos. I missed them more than anything. I used to drive to the San Gabriel Mountains every chance I got, just to be in the canyons up there—even though I had to share them with thousands of people. But it brought me a little bit of New Mexico."

Rudy is on his feet again, standing at the window, gazing off into the distance. He turns back, gesturing vaguely toward the view outside. "It's hard to describe the hold this place has on you. I was constantly importing things from New Mexico, trying to keep as much of it in our lives as possible. I used to rent a U-Haul trailer and take twenty-two sacks of green chile back to share with other New Mexicans."

He fires a question at me: "Do you know the one thing everybody always wanted from here?"

"Chile?"

"Wrong." He grins. "Baloney."

"Baloney?"

"Coronado brand baloney. That's one of the major things people export from New Mexico. You can't find it there. God, every time I'd go back I'd take ten or fifteen sticks of baloney for my friends."

"The *manitos*?"

He grins, surprised to hear me use the word. "You know about that? The *manitos*, the little brothers, the little people." He laughs. "There were a bunch of us there. We stuck together. But it wasn't the same thing. I tried planting chile in Pasadena and found that our variety of chile doesn't grow there. Against Pasadena city laws, I kept rabbits in the backyard. I did miss my way of life terribly.

"I finally came home in 1971 and it was just like being born again. For the first three years, I was worse than a tourist, rediscovering all these things I had taken for granted while I was growing up. That's when I started getting more involved with our traditions and our culture. Today I eat, sleep, and dream Hispanic culture."

"If your extended family had been down there with you, do you think you would have remained in California?"

"Never. I did have some friends and relatives in Los Angeles. But it wasn't right. I didn't really belong. Here, I look at the land as a brother, as a part of who I am, instead of just a piece of real estate, an investment. I longed to come back to my people, but it was also the land. I had left a good job here, but I wanted to come back with an education. It was one of my personal goals. It took me five years to complete four—because I had to work to support my family. I sacrificed because I wanted this thing so bad. At the time I was in school, I kept thinking, I can go back there and teach the guys in the area about auto repair. I mean, cars are a big deal here.

"The first thing I did here was work on the family cars." He rolls his eyes in a helpless gesture. "That almost became my whole life's work. On the Herrera side, I have seventy-three first cousins. Imagine how many offshoots there are. On the Gonzáles side there are forty-seven first cousins. As soon as all these relatives found out I was here and I was a mechanic with all this knowledge about automobiles, everybody started bringing their cars for tune-ups, overhauls, you name it. All I did for about a year was work for the family.

"I didn't want to go back into business. I wanted to teach or get into a salary-type job. But we have this obligation to our families. I got the family cars running fairly well—I mean, things that hadn't run for years were towed to the house—then I started concentrating on making a living."

Rudy was thankful to be home and loved the feeling of belonging, but he had trouble finding his niche. "I worked as a mechanic in Santa Fe. I went down to Cochiti Dam and helped construct some things there. Then I got called back to Los Alamos. It is

MECHANIC, LA PUEBLA

1950 FORD, POTRERO

CAR CLUB, ESPANOLA

ironic, but I went back to the same trade I'd left in 1962. The only difference was—and believe me it was a big difference—I had eleven years of experience under my belt, and I had a degree. That almost automatically put me into an administrative position. I didn't have to work with my hands very long."

A position of authority gave Rudy the opportunity to begin helping his people. "Seeing the Hispanics from northern New Mexico, the biggest majority of them working menial jobs, as janitors and laborers, woke something in me. I kept asking the question, 'Does a broom and a shovel only fit Hispanic and Indian hands? Don't the Anglo guys from Oklahoma or Ohio know how to work these tools?' I said to myself, 'Hey, I can help my people. I can help them better themselves. I can help them to take pride in their culture and traditions.' Which is one of the things that happens when you are a minority. You have a tendency to look down on yourself because somebody else is putting you down.

"At Los Alamos, I think I was instrumental in getting my people to look at themselves in a better light. I helped them to see that they were fortunate to have this culture and all these traditions. I worked to that end. I told them they could compete. I made some inroads and felt good about them, but it was an uphill grind.

"Finally, I knew it was time for me to leave. There was only so much I could do up there. Prejudice will always exist. It's a part of the human mind. I wanted to move on. It was time to enjoy my life. I wanted to devote my energy to researching and preserving this rich culture and these traditions."

BIKERS

The Second Law

The Entropy Law is the second law of thermodynamics. The first law states that all matter and energy in the universe is constant, that it cannot be created or destroyed. Only its form can be changed but never its essence. The second law, the Entropy Law, states that matter and energy can only be changed in one direction, that is, from the usable to the unusable, or from available to unavailable, or from ordered to disordered. In essence, the second law says that everything in the entire universe began with structure and value and is irrevocably moving in the direction of chaos and waste.

JEREMY RIFKIN

If it hadn't been for Los Alamos," Elfegio Baca begins, putting his car in drive and swinging out of the parking lot, "this would have been a sleepy town. All the young people would have split. But Los Alamos brings in a lot of money—salaries, federal funds for roads and education. It has made this place survive. But that is a two-edged sword. It has its good side and its bad side."

Elfegio is thin and self-possessed. He has high, sharply defined cheekbones, a pencil-thin mustache rides his curling lips, and he keeps his black hair cropped short. Perched on the bridge of his bladelike nose is a pair of expensive aviator sunglasses with mirrored lenses, the type favored by highway patrolmen.

A week ago, at the house of a mutual friend, Elfegio said he had a few things to say about his years of working at Los Alamos National Laboratories but that he wanted to do it in private. He finally decided we could talk in his car and asked me to meet him at the Furr's parking lot in Espanola. His car is new, a metallic blue Oldsmobile loaded with luxury features—power windows, cruise control, and custom leather seats that exude the rich smell of expensive hides. He drives out of Espanola, turns south at the new plaza, a grassy berm that bristles with flagpoles, and heads in the direction of Los Alamos.

The facility at Los Alamos is an anomaly. At first, its relatively inaccessible location—a place sequestered away from major metropolitan centers and convenient transportation routes—would appear to make it a poor choice as a site for a major scientific laboratory. But the isolation and secrecy were exactly what the government wanted when it selected that particular site.

Los Alamos, Spanish for "the cottonwoods," is situated on the remote Pajarito Plateau to the southwest of Espanola. Its history extends back to a time before the bomb, a time before the Spaniards. The Pajarito Plateau served as the hunting ground for the ancestral Tewa Indians. About A.D. 1100 they began building their villages on it. However, by the sixteenth century the Indians abandoned these villages. It is thought that, not unlike many other tribes in the area, the Tewas were forced to migrate to lower ground by a shrinking moisture base. Whatever the reason, they left and established new villages closer to the rivers.

During the nineteenth and twentieth centuries both Hispanics and Anglos used the land on the plateau for cattle and sheep ranching. They cut the trees for lumber and, with little success, tried mining. Hispanics especially found the soil well suited to dryland farming—beans was a principle crop. Families from the valley camped on the plateau during the summers, though few located residences there.

Then, in 1918, Ashley Pond, who had come to New Mexico from Michigan, acquired land on the plateau and founded the Los Alamos Ranch School, a venture far different from any previously attempted on the hill. Pond was an idealist and his school, for boys only, was formulated on principles that brought together a healthy life in the out-of-doors and a curriculum modeled on the classics. The rugged ranch setting, with horseback riding and camping, a challenging array of classes put together by the school's impressive faculty, and teachers handpicked from the best Eastern universities, appealed to the mostly wealthy parents who sent their sons there—as did the hearty, dry climate and, of course, the protective isolation of New Mexico.

In 1942, after the school had been operating for more than two decades, a group of army officers stopped by to inform Pond, through his headmaster Albert Connell, that the government would be buying the Los Alamos Ranch School. It was an order, simple and firm. Protest had absolutely no effect. The government offered Pond fair compensation for the land, buildings, and everything else. He needed only disband the school, pack his personal effects, and leave. The U.S. government expected to assume ownership immediately. Pond and his people had no recourse.

By 1943 Dr. Robert Oppenheimer had moved onto the hill along with a number of other scientists and technical personnel. Work was begun at the lab that would eventually become the home of the bomb. From the beginning, Los Alamos National Laboratories' existence and purpose was shrouded in secrecy, a status that continued for decades before it was gradually lifted. Today, the huge complex of scientific facilities, many of which are concealed by trees and the camouflage of the natural terrain, remains primarily a stronghold controlled by outsiders.

Elfegio rolls up his shirtsleeves as he drives through Santa Clara Pueblo. His forearms are sinewy and well-muscled, his hands callused from the farm work he does in his spare time. He asks if I'd like a Coke and then nods toward a Styrofoam cooler in the backseat. There was a time, not so long ago, when we'd have been drinking beer—maybe accompanied by shots of tequila—but Elfegio has quit drinking. I recall his account of the incident that brought him to his decision. After a long night in the Espanola bars, he rode his Harley-Davidson home in a driving rainstorm and brought the machine to a stop beside his house. As he was trying to get the kickstand down, his foot slipped on the greasy clay and the bike fell, pinning him beneath it. The rain was turning to snow. He was too drunk to move the bike. He struggled and finally passed out. Early the next morning his wife found him, covered with snow and chilled to the bone; with her help, he extracted himself from under the motorcycle and limped into the house.

"If you are Hispanic and you work on the hill," he begins, "you are expected automatically to give up a lot of your cultural roots. That's just understood. A few years ago it was even worse. My father worked up there then and the bosses refused to pronounce the peculiar Spanish names like Florencio, Melaquias, Agustín, and my own name, Elfegio. As a consequence, everyone from down here with that kind of name became Joe. It was an insult, but his generation conformed to it. My father joked that he had been baptized José. I guess it is true in a certain sense because all of us feel we are Joseph and Mary.

"So right from the beginning, the powers that be in Los Alamos have discriminated against the people from the valley. We were never thought to be competent enough to do anything except service the machine. A lot of the inferiority feelings the people here have come from just that, forever doing service work. But there is no other game in town. People used to farm, but farming doesn't pay. So you just say yes-sir-boss and go with the flow. You put up with the discrimination and the abuse because you would rather be working than not working."

"What do you mean by 'abuse'?"

He runs a finger over the thin line of his mustache. "Part of it has to do with trapping you in your job, making you a slave to it. The bosses like the idea of seeing you buy a new car or a house because then you've got to come to work and be a good boy. Once I made the mistake of telling my boss that I didn't have to be there, that I could do something else for a living. He's a career man and he definitely did not want to hear that."

"But you've stayed on the job."

"Yes, I've just celebrated ten years of full-time employment at the lab, which gives me a total of fourteen years, counting the part-time work I did during the time I was going to school, and during all that time I've never felt that I belonged up there. I'm feeling it even more now."

"On the one hand," I say, "you describe the discrimination you feel and I hear bitterness. But on the other hand you tell me that you've worked up there all these years and I detect a note of pride in your voice."

Lowriders, near Chimayo

This produces a smile. He settles back in the leather seat. "I can say that I am proud of what I have done at the lab. But how far can I go up there? It's a closed-end future. As a Hispanic, you can start at point A and perhaps make it to about point M, which I call mediocrity. You can go to work every day, never piss anybody off, and move up through the system to that point. But that's your limit. The lab likes to claim they're seeking achievers, people who'll make a difference, people who'll excel. But that isn't true, at least not as far as Hispanics are concerned. Those are the very people they punish. They won't allow you to stick out that far. Too many employees are worried about their positions and they don't want any competition for them. The system at the lab makes sure that nobody gets too far ahead because that kind of individuality disrupts the normal rhythm of the organization."

"What's behind the insecurity?" I ask.

"The whole intellectual climate up there," he says without hesitation. "Los Alamos is really just a university town. It has a university mentality. It is hung up on education and insecure because of it."

The temperature inside the car has risen, and Elfegio turns on the air-conditioning.

"I'm not sure I understand," I tell him.

"The people throw their credentials at you. And you can't be anything unless you have the better paper. You can't just be a good chemist. You have to be a good chemist from such-and-such university."

Beyond Black Mesa, which looms on the left, we swing west onto the Los Alamos highway. The road winds through a series of sharp switchbacks. Elfegio slows behind a truck, waits for an approaching car to go by, then shoots out into the left lane and passes.

"The lab brings in experts from the outside, from the major universities, the navy, the Department of Energy—lots of bigwigs who treat the lab like a pit stop. They recognize the value of coming here. But they don't want to be here forever." I hear the bitterness in his voice. "They come in to use us. We are there to serve them. They take from us but they don't feel they need to respect us because to them we are the cheap labor force. If anything great happens—even if we do the work and make it happen on our own—they take the credit. In their eyes we're just maintenance people, nothing more. We're never allowed entry into the private club with the outsiders. And I resent that."

He shrugs. "I guess basically what I have is a deep resentment about the lab. In business, the person who excels, who gets out and hustles and is innovative, is rewarded for his efforts. In the university environment that's not true. To these people, the smartest person in the room is supposedly the most highly educated person, regardless of how inept he is at putting what he knows to work."

"Have you expressed these feelings to your bosses?"

He smiles slightly. "Up there you learn that it's best to keep your comments to yourself. And I guess that is where I run into problems. I like the freedom to speak my mind. I like the freedom to come and go and delve into the things I want to get into. It's pretty idealistic, I guess, and it has caused me some trouble."

"You could do other things, right?"

"Yes."

"You could go someplace else and work, right?"

The disparity between his words—and the values they reflect—and his actions seems obvious and I ask bluntly why he bothers to stay, why he has remained working at the lab for fourteen years.

"It's a cushy job," he says. "Where else can you go to work and get paid for not doing too much? There are three of you to do the work of one. That's why people up there defend their jobs so vigorously and put up with so much shit and discrimination. There are perks. But they have helped to create a lot of low self-esteem."

Hundreds of people from the Espanola Valley work on the hill, but few choose to live there. To them it is another world, both intellectually and physically different from the rest of northern New Mexico. It resembles, instead, communities in Silicon Valley or Marin County, near San Francisco.

"Los Alamos has every amenity that you find in a big city," Elfegio says. He is speaking now as a person from the valley, but he is hardly ignorant of the outside world. He went away to school; he has traveled. "The lab offers better equipment and facilities than most major universities. It has to have it in order to attract the caliber of people it needs.

And then it has us, the peons, to serve these people and clean up after them when they're done.

"And that's our problem. We can't break out of that mold. Which creates frustration and resentment. You want to stand up and cry out to the bosses: *Hey, I'm here. I'm just as good. Listen to me. I can work.* But they never forget that you are Hispanic, and to them that means Mexican."

"How can discrimination be so blatant?" I ask. "We have laws to protect workers against that kind of treatment."

He laughs at my naivete. "They satisfy the laws. The employment office sets up this facade of being an Equal Opportunity Employer. They've got a token minority sitting there behind a desk to prove it. He's a yes boy. He says what they want to hear, enough to satisfy any government investigator. But there is no equal opportunity anything up here. It's only politics in a different form. It's frustrating for someone who wants to be recognized for his own abilities."

"You feel it?"

"Yes. If I'd come from Kansas or New York or someplace it would be different. It is a curse being born in the valley—unless you get out. It's a stigma we can't escape."

"Do you think it is the same for this generation of kids?"

"Yes. They feel the futility."

The road snakes along the side of a canyon and climbs to the top of the plateau. A cluster of buildings to the right houses various contractors to the lab. Beyond them is the airport, its runway sweeping dramatically to the edge of the plateau. Elfegio has brought me here to share his thoughts. I realize that they nag at him each day he makes this drive. It is not difficult to see Los Alamos from Elfegio's point of view. Little about it resembles any part of the valley. It is planned and orderly, the buildings low and strictly functional, their predominant color the gray of mothballed ships, the homes built in the California style. They are surrounded by those yards Hilario Romero labeled as typical gringo creations—lawns that have to be watered and mowed, separated by fences or hedges that have to be clipped.

I suggest that there must be other people in Los Alamos, people not from the valley, who share his feelings.

"Maybe," he concedes. "But I have a hard time with the people up here. They have no roots. Most of them can pack up within thirty days and leave. It takes a certain type of person who can continually move and never get tied down to anything."

"There are people who have lived here for years, who consider themselves as having roots up here."

"I don't want to talk against those people but it isn't the same. I mean family. But that's only my view because I have roots in New Mexico that go back for generations. I have gone out. I have traveled. And I am glad to return to what I have here. I see people on the hill who come and go and have no loyalties to their fellow man or anything else, including their families. They are loyal to their work and that is as far as it goes. They fool around and get divorced and their home life changes, but their work remains constant. Their lives do not center around their families. They seem to have no loyalties or self-respect, because to get ahead in their field they'll do anything."

There appears to be little purpose to his driving through the town, other than to jog his memory. He is silent for a few moments. We pass a complex of stores.

"I can't deny that the lab has been good for me," he begins, a note of acquiescence in his voice. "I have recommended it to my friends. They've gotten jobs here and they seem content. Now they have a place to roost. Myself, I have been disillusioned by it. It is not what it seems. The bosses tell you that you can be what you want, but they don't allow it to happen."

He turns onto Trinity heading east, back toward the valley. The Saturday traffic moves smoothly, the flow of cars thinning out as we move past the airport.

"This is what I wait for every day." He gestures at the panorama unfolding before the car, a sweep of country that opens up with the Espanola Valley and reaches all the way to the Sangre de Cristo Mountains. "This is what makes it so I can keep working up here."

"I hear that the lab is cutting back, eliminating people," I say. "Does that worry you? Do you wonder if you'll have a job next year, or the year after?"

"No."

"If it did happen, would you leave the valley?"

CROSSES, WEST OF SANTUARIO

"I'd have to cross that bridge when I came to it," he says.

"So you have no concern about it?"

"No. I believe the lab is going to grow. The nuclear industry in the United States and the world is going to grow—even with the threat of nuclear waste."

"Do you see the waste as a problem?"

"It is a problem—but not for us, for me. Nobody wants it," he says, with a sardonic smile. "But New Mexico will take it. They will take the plutonium and put it somewhere. Give our politicians a few thousand bucks and they'll roll over. That attitude is a stigma we all have to live up to. Remember that bargeful of New York City garbage that nobody wanted? Somebody in our state government was actually talking about bringing it here. What the hell, right?"

His attitude disturbs me. "What about you? Aren't you concerned for the safety of your family?"

"I believe in nuclear," he says. "I believe it is what we should be doing in this country and I don't think it is ultimately all that dangerous."

"People are talking about the risk of cancer from contamination at the lab. They're pointing to whole neighborhoods where the number of cases is elevated many times above the national average."

"They're just playing with statistics. People could fall asleep for three months in the levels of radiation that we work around before they would ever be affected. Very few people involved in radiation work can be killed by radiation."

This statement seems irresponsible and I tell him so.

He disagrees. "The immediate danger up here would be getting cut and then absorbing the stuff into your bloodstream. Any real danger would be for subsequent generations."

"Isn't that important?"

"Of course. But we don't know that it is there."

Plutonium, one of the actinides, which occur naturally in only miniscule amounts, was made in larger quantities when Glenn Seaborg, along with Macmillan, Kennedy, and Wahl, effected a successful deuteron bombardment of uranium in 1940. Plutonium is an alpha-particle emitter and can be absorbed into the bones. As such, it is potentially hazardous. I remind him of that danger.

But Elfegio is adamant. "If I got cut at work and took on a dose, a body burden, as we call it, it's not going to kill me. I'm going to die of natural causes before it hurts me. It takes a long time for those effects to hit you."

"What about the groundwater? We hear that it is being poisoned by the unprotected dumps. Nobody even remembers where any of them are located."

"That is a different problem."

"But it is happening and that should concern you."

"The people of Hiroshima were subjected to enormous fallout. They got it on them. They breathed it. There were horrific examples of mutogenesis. The gene structure was altered. The worst effects didn't come out until the next generation. But it is not going to affect me unless I have a child after I've been exposed. Then maybe it will manifest itself and maybe it won't. Very few people at the lab are exposed to enough radiation to alter their gene structure. We deal mostly in low-level stuff. For security reasons no one is allowed to have enough to make a bomb. That is the real threat. Even if you have a bomb you can make a bang, but it probably won't hurt you as far as radiation is concerned. Safeguards are in place to keep that kind of exposure at a minimum."

"Are you telling me that a person can't be affected by radiation?"

"In our situation it is minimal. We do have some reactors that are bad because they are high neutron and gamma emitters. You know, megadoses. But those places are well shielded. They are not constantly online. They are brought up basically for photographic purposes, to see how metal is altered. But the people who use them are so well protected that there is no danger."

"And you keep insisting that radiation is not that dangerous?"

Elfegio clarifies his position. "Radiation is not that dangerous in our situation—because we always know where it's at. An electric wire is more dangerous because it can kill you. Plutonium can't kill you unless someone forms it into a hammer and beats you over the head with it. In the whole history of the lab only two people have died due to plutonium exposure. And there was a lot of negligence involved. People like to target us, but we are nothing compared to the microchip and petrochemical industries. They are constantly coming out with new forms of chemicals they don't know how to get rid of. They transport that stuff out on the highways constantly. They have spills. Towns are evacuated, cleanup crews come in, and they just hope to hell the wind carries off the fumes. Those are real threats. If a truck loaded with plutonium wrecked and every container broke open, you wouldn't feel it or taste it or anything. It wouldn't even discolor the road."

His reasoning makes me uneasy. "What I hear you saying is that you have sold out."

He bristles. "Plutonium is not that dangerous," he repeats. "I've been involved in the analysis of plutonium. I know a little about it and its nature and it is not that harmful."

"And if you get it in your bloodstream?"

"Then you don't know what it's going to do."

"That's my point."

"Still, it's not going to kill you."

"What about cancer?"

"There is that danger. But cancer is rampant. Everything is cancer. There were people at the beginning of work up here who handled plutonium and ingested it but they never actually died from it. We've had people at the lab who've had accidents and been killed, but they were involved with major solutions that inadvertently produced a lot of neutrons."

"So you are saying that it is dangerous."

Elfegio drives on in silence. He signals and turns off the Los Alamos highway toward Espanola. Finally he says, "The stress of worrying about radiation has killed more people than actual radiation. But the way we handle plutonium at the lab, in those quantities, it is in itself not that dangerous. I'm not saying that it is completely safe. What is? Grab an electric wire and it's going to hurt you. Light a match around gas and it's going to blow. Radiation's the same. If you take precautions, it's not going to hurt you. It's when people deviate from procedures that they get hurt. The more people involved, the more chances you have of a screwup. Most of the accidents we've had have to do with the workers, not the science."

I am beginning to realize that, in spite of his objections, he has bought the lab's propaganda, that he is more a part of it than he will admit. How many others like him will turn a blind eye to the hazards as long as the paycheck keeps coming? "What is it about the job that keeps you there? Is it simply that it's a 'cushy' job?"

"The real beauty of the lab," he begins, more relaxed that I am no longer challenging his stand, "is having the chance to work with things that are available almost nowhere else. We have one of the biggest and fastest computers in the world. We have library facilities that can access every kind of material a scientist would require."

"Yet you began by telling me how stymied you were by the lab, how it held you down, how it discriminated."

"It does, and I hate that part. But put it this way: I have a good forum to do something up there. I've already published one paper. I'm getting ready to do another one. The system stinks, but I'm going to use it. I've learned. I've used equipment I'd never have seen if I hadn't been up there."

"At one time, by your own admission, you would have considered what you just told me 'selling out.'"

"That's true. But I changed my tactics."

"And your values?"

He pulls alongside my car, which I left in the Furr's parking lot. He leaves the engine running, cool air pumping from the air conditioner. "From here on out, I'm going to play the game. Recently I was part of a forum where my technical expertise and abilities made it possible for me to join a safety committee. Safety is a huge concern at the lab. Now I travel and represent the lab. I'm getting some respect." He obviously feels good about this.

"Is that enough?"

"I don't know. It's more than I had. I've learned how to pace myself. I used to think they wanted someone to work for them. I gave them all I had and it seemed they didn't want that. I didn't get any farther than the guy who just stuck his feet up on the desk and told his boss he was busy."

"And what is your future? How far can you go up there?"

"I said it before: Hispanics can only get so far at the lab. New Mexico is never going to supply anything more than the trades and maintenance people—maybe a few others, like myself, who somehow slipped through a loophole. But I'm not kidding myself. I can only go so far. I know it."

"They don't call you Joe."

"No. I've made a little headway. But I could never live long enough to see a native New Mexican become head of the lab. Regardless of your race, you could be the most qualified guy in the world and they would pass you over."

"Because you are from New Mexico."

"They always go for the guy who comes from out of state. They'll hire him for twice the money as long as he's not from here."

"And you don't think that'll ever change."

"Never."

Jewelry Maker, Hernandez

Relating to the Revolt

In the transmission of human culture, people always
attempt to replicate, to pass on to the next generation
the skills and values of the parents; but the attempt
always fails because cultural transmission is geared
to learning, not to DNA.

GREGORY BATESON

Paul is one of those morning commuters out of the north who arrives in Santa Fe just after seven forty-five in order to be at his desk by eight, the hour the state of New Mexico officially begins its workday. There are two posters on the wall facing his desk, one by Georgia O'Keeffe advertising the Santa Fe Opera, the other an abstraction from the Museum of New Mexico.

Paul invites me to sit down and then replies to my first question with no hesitation. "I have a solid formal education, which is something I used to believe in. I always thought that was what I needed to make it. Now I wonder if it's ever going to help me accomplish the things I want to do."

"What changed your mind?"

"I took a hard look at my priorities. I realized that my traditional life is the most important thing to me. In the pueblos there is a calling for the educated people to try and preserve Indian life. I accept that. But for me there is a conflict. On the one hand, I feel the urge to record our history and make it so the non-Indian world can understand who we are. I always saw my education as essential to that goal. On the other hand, I think what I should really be doing is helping our young people learn the traditions."

"Does the conflict come because of pressure from your native religion?" I ask.

"No. There is no pressure there. Our religion isn't forced on us. The people who come to our beliefs, which is a whole complete way of life, do it of their own free will. The calling is to everyone. It's not like a religion where a preacher is singled out to devote his life as a leader. Each of our people has it. Religion in our life is a constant. Unlike the Protestant or Catholic who goes to church on Sunday and then turns around on Monday and beats his wife, we are expected to live our religion twenty-four hours a day, seven days a week. Once you accept the Indian way, it governs everything you do. There are different steps. You take on certain obligations in different clans and different groups. Maybe you are in a singing group or a medicine clan or a drumming clan. Whatever, you take a step beyond the ordinary. Then you go deeper; you make a bigger commitment. You take it to levels where you devote your entire existence to the traditional lifestyle. Anything in the outside world becomes secondary. I have felt that pull toward total commitment; but I've resisted it because I believe my first responsibility is for me to use my gift to work with the young people and make the Indian world stronger."

"What about the young people in the tribes, do you see them leaning toward the traditional values or are they falling away?"

"It depends on the village. In some they are stronger, in others they are losing it. I believe it's all based on the example of the older people. The old people like to blame the kids for not carrying on our traditions, but the reason they don't have the traditions is the fault of the older people. They are the ones who should set the example. They should take responsibility. But they like somebody to blame. That shows there is something missing in they way the elders carry on their kiva traditions. Strong villages exist because parents and elders set a good example, they make an effort to involve their children in the life."

"Which are the strong villages?"

"Oh, God"—he laughs—"that is a loaded question. But I'll be honest. Santo Domingo is one of the stronger villages."

Santo Domingo lies to the southwest of Santa Fe. It is a large pueblo, well known for its jewelry and crafts, home to perhaps the largest groups of dancers in the Southwest.

"San Ildefonso, which is my village, I admire for being very modern in its approach to the outside world, in accepting the luxuries of the world and still maintaining a traditional lifestyle. That is something to be proud of, but in the process of achieving it we have also lost a lot. And our elders tell me that once something is lost from the tradition it is gone forever.

"Indian tradition is woven of a delicate yet surprisingly durable fabric. Things can evolve, they can change. Our people accept that change. But if a song from someone's family is lost, you cannot just suddenly bring it back. That song is gone. The only way to preserve those things is to educate the young people about the values of our life. If you can't motivate them to continue the traditions then there is nothing you can do."

"Can't they be recorded?"

"That's one solution. But it is an Anglo solution. You can write them down. You can copy them and put them on tape. But I think that they lose some of their value when you do that."

"So what you are saying is that once a song is out of the strictly oral tradition it is no longer as strong."

Despite Paul's education and sophistication, his cautious view stems from a reluctance to trust the tools of the electronic age, to commit sacred and venerable material to something as impersonal as a tape recorder. It is less a mistrust of the machine than knowledge that the process of repetition and memorization assures the reverence necessary to preservation of sense and feeling as well as the literal text.

"I hope we'll never get to the point in our village where we'll need to record a song to make sure we don't lose it. I'd hate to have to make the decision that that was what we needed."

I was curious about the decision-making at Paul's pueblo. The *Rio Grande Sun* had published a story about a power struggle among the leaders at San Ildefonso. I ask Paul to clarify it for me.

"We have some internal political problems in the pueblo," he admits freely. "We've got this guy who became power hungry. He thought that being governor gave him some kind of ultimate power. Rather than serving the people, as he should have done, he seems to think he is going to control the people. Where he came up with that idea I don't know. It's completely opposite from our basic philosophy. It's disturbing, you know. We thought we had a leader who was going to do a lot for the pueblo but he's turned out to be this power-hungry maniac. Right now we are trying to get rid of him. Unfortunately, what we are having to do is employ Anglo methods of getting him out. We have to do that because that's the way the Bureau of Indian Affairs has structured our tribal government. We have to follow their procedures in order to impeach him."

"What will that do to the village?"

"Nothing of value. We've had some struggles lately that have eroded the system. It is amazing how this external political force, based on the Anglo model, can eat at the traditional structure of a village. Only the stronger villages come out intact. It happened down in Isleta and out in Zuni. At Zuni an opposing group stole all the canes of authority, the symbols of tribal leadership. It was almost war, but they made it through. Only because they are a strong village.

"The story of Isleta is pretty interesting. They had a woman for governor, which was unbelievable for that pueblo. She was doing a great job. Then a couple of men who were bitter for some reason decided they wanted to get rid of her. They started a smear campaign against her. She used the system to help her, and she won the battle. So maybe there is hope for us."

"Doesn't this all smack of a double standard?"

"Yes. There is a definite double standard because we have to accept due process and the Bill of Rights and that whole rigmarole. But that has had its benefits. On a purely traditional level there are villages where, good or bad, women are not allowed to vote. But the traditional system had its own checks and balances. In it every person held a certain place on a level of importance. Everyone had his or her input in some way or other. But it seems to me that because we have accepted the double standard, as you put it, and imposed the non-Indian government on our people while we still retain the traditional government, there is bound to be some confusion, some gray areas. Still, we have to deal with the outsiders. We cannot deal with them in the kiva because outsiders are not allowed to participate. So we have to deal with them on a level that they can understand. Sadly, we have not been very successful at making people understand who we are.

"One thing I really get tired of is tourists looking at our villages like they were these miniature Disneylands where they can come in and gawk and do whatever they want. Don't get me wrong. We welcome people. We welcome visitors. There has never been a point in our history when we've shut them out of our villages. But, please, come and enjoy them for what they are. Respect our way of life. Don't try to make us into something we aren't. Don't ask us to be your noble savage. Anglos never looked at us as *civilized*, though we've been far more civilized for a longer period of time than the Anglos. Look at our ancestors, the Anasazi and the Hohokam. They had cultures with elaborate life systems that included politics, religion, horticulture, and complex social structures."

"Have the impositions made by the BIA [Bureau of Indian Affairs] significantly weakened the traditional tribal structure?"

"You base your faith on what you know and how well it works, and if the tradition is still working, which it is, then you know that there is something to it. You have to see the saving grace. Like justice in America." He pauses to smile. "I have seen the traditional principles weather through time when the whole tribal system seemed on the point of collapse. We are not alone in our problems. Santa Clara, whose clans have been at each other's throats for years, continues to survive. I see the same thing in all the cultures of the valley. You have Hispanics there who keep alive this DeVargas the Conqueror attitude. That stuff went out of style a long time ago. They need to move on to something more positive. But they hold on to it for dear life, like it's the only thing they've got. They measure their worth and power from that distant point in time. The whole idea is so minuscule, so pathetic. It's that macho trip all over again."

"Speaking about the Spanish, would it be fair to say that your people have preserved certain aspects of your culture by taking the beliefs and practices imposed upon you by outsiders and assuming them like a veneer?"

"Veneer is an interesting concept," he says. "I can see how it has worked with Catholicism, for example. Indians love ceremony, which is one reason the Catholic

Memorial, near San Juan Pueblo

La Conquistadora, Garden,
Santuario de Chimayo

Church was so successful in the pueblos. There was this guy, this priest, with these costumes and glitter and the big shining metal cross and everything. He stood up in front and wanted to lead. We were in awe of that, although few people ever fully accepted the doctrines. They said, 'Hey, this looks pretty good, let's see what's going on.'

"My grandmother was a good Catholic and a good Indian. She put them together and made them work. To me they are contradictions. I embrace the Indian religion; I do not embrace the Catholic Church. I accept my people accepting it and criticize no one for doing it. I just find it hard personally to be both a Catholic and an Indian. Most outside religion boils down to saying if you don't believe in the church you are going to go to hell. That is something we never do. If you don't go to the kiva, well, you don't go to the kiva. You miss out on what is being offered, but no one is going to tell you you're going to hell because you missed it."

A smile surfaces. "Maybe part of the reason Indians seem to accept the Catholic Church is that we are practical people. We want to cover all the bases. We're playing it safe. Just in case our religion isn't up to snuff, just in case God really is a Catholic." He laughs.

Paul's mention of the Catholic Church is significant. Indians transformed it. They took what the priests offered and, without substantially altering the surface appearances, created their own church. The Franciscans, eager for a trade-off, watched this happen. They even encouraged the changes, so long as overall appearances were maintained; in that way, they made significant inroads into the villages. The result was more converts who could be counted and whose numbers could be conveyed back to the king.

Often, however, there were priests whose methods showed little or no respect for the Indian people. They used them as slaves, abused them, and appropriated their lands. The Spaniards continued to make progress, adding converts to their rolls, keeping the pueblos under control—until, finally, they pressed too hard. The Indians grew resentful. They went underground. In 1680 the tension that had grown steadily against the Spaniards triggered the Great Pueblo Revolt.

I ask Paul what view the Pueblos take of the revolt.

"A proud part of history," he declares, "a part of history that needs telling. When I saw *Dances With Wolves* I felt I was seeing the rewriting of American history. There have been plenty of great books like *Black Elk Speaks* and *Son of the Morning Star,* books from both my people and the Anglos. I see all this as a starting point. People in the United States are beginning to learn their real history. It angers me that people refuse to deal with the truth, with reality. We're not out of the woods, but this is a beginning. The news media manipulate situations for government favor. News is all glossed over and glamorized, a big commercial endeavor. In an effort to show the sensational action they trivialize anything significant.

"The Spaniards tried to do that to our holy men. It was the last straw. It brought on the revolt."

The revolt was the brainchild of Pope, a holy man from San Juan Pueblo. In 1675, along with forty-seven other medicine men, Pope was incarcerated in Santa Fe. They were accused of sorcery and witchcraft because they continued to teach the traditional beliefs of the kiva, beliefs that did not include the Spanish God. Three of the elders were killed and the others were beaten and tortured. Pope himself was flogged and then released. Craving revenge and restitution, he began a campaign to avenge all wrongs inflicted on the Indian people by the Spaniards.

"The revolt is the only time the Indian people really changed their philosophy of life—as far as aggressive action goes," Paul says. "All through history we have engaged in little battles or skirmishes. You could hardly call them wars. A few people got killed, others were clubbed. Nothing like the mass slaughters Europeans brought about under the name of Christianity. So for the first time in our history we became so uncharacteristically aggressive that we did really inhuman things. We killed priests. We hanged them from their churches. We burned churches. In the pueblos, no matter how bad things got, I don't think we would attack somebody's kiva. That is contrary to Indian nature.

"The revolt was something else. It came at a time when people were saying, 'We are tired of this mistreatment. Our way of life has endured for thousands of years and we are tired of these people telling us we are wrong. We are tired of people killing our religious leaders. We are tired of priests and soldiers coming into our kivas and destroying the symbols of what we believe is the most important part of our lives.' So what we had was a religious war. Of course, it is rarely depicted that way. The simple truth is Indians were being persecuted for their religious beliefs and they were fed up with it."

There were serious grievances. The Spaniards were bent on undermining the Indians' religious life. At the root of the conflict, too, was a long history of the violation of a number of rights and personal freedoms. The Spaniards had enslaved the Indians, they had appropriated their property, and they had forced themselves sexually upon Indian women and boys.

After almost a century the Spaniards had been only marginally successful in their campaign to convert Indians en masse to the church. Out of frustration grew a bitterness toward a people they clearly failed to understand. Nothing they did convinced the Indians of their own inherent wickedness, nor persuaded them to believe in the Spaniards' superior virtues. As a result, tribal medicine men gained renewed strength among their people. The Spaniards reacted, imposing more drastic measures to bring the Indians under control.

After Pope was released he returned to San Juan and initiated a secret campaign against the Spaniards. His plan met with opposition from Francisco Xavier, a San Juan official openly sympathetic to the Spaniards. When it became clear to Pope that he would be unable to operate from his home pueblo, he went north to Taos. Legend has it that there, in an *estufa,* or kiva, he began lengthy communications with three spirits— Caudi, Tilim, and Tlueme. At the same time he established a network among the tribes under Spanish rule. He and the others met in secret and formulated a plan. At a precise moment on a given day, the Indians were to seize and kill every Spaniard they could find, take their guns and ammunition, and thus arm themselves for war. They were to spare no one, including women, children, and missionaries.

Even though the planning had been carried out in secret, the chain of trust was uncertain. Among those the architects of the revolt considered capable of leaking the plan to the Spaniards was Pope's own son-in-law, Nicolás Bua, governor of San Juan Pueblo. To ensure his silence, he was killed.

In Paul's view the revolt set an important precedent. "It instilled in us an approach to how we can deal with the non-Indian. We realized then that we have something worth fighting for, something worth protecting, and we are going to do it no matter what the consequences. Even though the revolt wasn't depicted that way in the printed histories, it has always been talked about that way in the kivas."

The plan Pope and the other leaders formulated to announce the start of the revolt was to present a knotted cord to the tribes joined in the conspiracy. The knots were to be untied until none remained; on the day the final knot was untied the action would begin. Various modern-day authors have determined that date to be August 10, 11, or 13. Their information in this as in all other things comes strictly from Spanish sources who relied upon Indians loyal to the Spaniards or from those Indians from whom the Spaniards coerced their information. The Indian voice is typically silent.

Not surprisingly, the Indians involved in the conspiracy found it impossible to cleave together. The chiefs of three pueblos informed Governor Otermin in Santa Fe that two Tesuque Indians, Catua and Omtua, had brought word of the revolt. The two messengers were taken to Santa Fe and made to confess that the remaining two knots in the cord meant the revolt was to take place in as many days.

The capture of the messengers sounded an alarm among the people of Tesuque. According to the confession forced from Pedro Naranjo, a captive Indian identified as a member of the Keres nation, the tribes decided to move up the attack. Word of this was circulated by another set of messengers and the revolt began at daybreak of the following day, August 10. The government, lacking full knowledge of the scope of the revolt and the number of Indians involved, acted with too little speed to stem the onslaught. Otermin dispatched men to caution nearby villagers, but the warning came too late and most were left victim to a massacre the extent of which they could never have imagined.

The first Spaniard to be killed was Cristóbal Herrera. He was murdered at the Tesuque Pueblo on the night of August 9. The subsequent slaughter of Spaniards by the Indians is recorded in vivid detail—at least in those cases where survivors came forth to testify.

In part, the Indians were successful because of the clever use of misinformation. Otermin was made to believe that his allies to the south had perished. He was given the choice to leave, which he rejected. He fought back the Indians with a force of barely one hundred armed men. However, once he realized that more Indians were descending on the capital from the north, he fled with his people, taking them south to the Isleta Pueblo, which had not joined in the revolt. Realizing they would not be safe there, he took them, together with a number of the faithful Indians, and decamped farther south to El Paso. It was sixteen years later before the Spaniards, now under the leadership of Don Diego DeVargas, were able once again to take control of the territory.

Blame for the revolt is often laid on Pope. To discredit the whole thing, it has been implied that he acted out of personal grievance, that he was a wild man who invented the story of the three spirits in the kiva at Taos merely to inflame the Indians. Those responsible for such arguments fail to take into account that the revolt came after five years of planning or that it occurred as the result of more than eight decades of Spanish injustice toward the Indians. These were people who had been abused, who had experienced hunger, people whose dignity had been attacked time after time.

"During the revolt is probably the first time the Pueblos were ever unified in anything," Paul declares. "Even then they made mistakes. They didn't know how to work together. Otherwise they would have wiped out the Spaniards totally. There would have been no slipups, no mistakes.

"The truth is, the tribes are all radically different, separate. We have no connections other than the fact that we speak Tewa. We don't even like to think about a connection. We are that individualized in our villages.

"In the old days it was even worse. If someone from my village married someone from Santa Clara, which you know is only a few miles away, the people said he was marrying outside. It was like marrying a non-Indian. Our people view it as the same thing. It wasn't that you were marrying another Indian. You were marrying an outsider.

"We are very tribe-oriented. I try not to be that way because it seems so petty. But one time someone wrote in the newspaper that I was from Santo Domingo and I was really upset. I called the writer and said, 'If you can't get anything else right, you could at least get which village I'm from.' The guy said, 'Aren't you a Pueblo Indian?' I said, 'That's what you call us, but I'm a San Ildefonso.'

"Let me give you another example. Once I agreed to dance at Santa Clara to satisfy an obligation I had. I thought, well, I'll get through this, but the experience was jarring. It was easy enough to pick up on the songs. The dance was similar to our corn dance. However, the way they did things in the kiva and certain inflections in the songs made me feel uncomfortable, like I was in another place altogether.

"I can go to Zia, where they speak Keres. Even there some of the ceremonies are very much like ours. Some of their songs and dances and even their costumes are similar to ours, but I see the difference. I can believe that an anthropologist, an outsider, who has studied these dances for years would never see that difference. He has looked at the dances for ten years maybe and he still misses the details — because he's not a part of any of the cultures. But I see them. It all goes back to our learning process. The dance, the ceremony, the Indian way of life is not something you understand from a book. It's something you have to get from real experience. That experience tells you how different we all are. That is why the revolt was so amazing. There is a whole world of difference between Taos, where Pope went to live, and San Juan, where he was from."

"But you acknowledge that there is a basic common thread that ties all the tribes together."

"No," he says, "there is a basic thread that ties us all to the world."

CHURCH, ESTACA

Bringing the World to the Tradition

My home over there, my home over there,
My home over there, now I remember it!

TEWA SONG

The landscape south of Espanola is dominated by Black Mesa. Known to the Tewa as Tunjopin, this magnificent plateau, rising like an ancient tower at the southern end of the valley, appears to have uncanny control over light and color. During the early part of the day it absorbs light, assimilating it and gradually growing darker and more varied in hue; then, in late afternoon, it begins to radiate back a spectrum of deep, brooding color. As light moves around it, patterns of shadow on its surface shift radically to make Black Mesa appear to be constantly reshaping itself, as though it were slowly spinning and dancing in place.

Santa Clara Pueblo, like its sister pueblos in the valley, San Juan and San Ildefonso, lies not far from the Rio Grande. Elevated on a hill above the west bank of the river, it has a commanding view of Black Mesa and the whole Sangre de Cristo range. When dawn breaks on early summer mornings, the disk of the sun, as seen from the pueblo, is said to rise out of the Sangre de Cristos in a spot the Tewa have called the Gap of the Sun.

The entrances to Santa Clara bristle with clusters of crosses erected in remembrance of tribal members who have died on that section of the highway between Espanola and

Los Alamos. At the heart of the pueblo are the buildings of an ancient Santa Clara, structures put up centuries ago. Tacked on around them are the newer sections of the pueblo, added since the 1960s, that consist of the same BIA-sponsored tract housing one sees at San Juan, with its boxlike design, aluminum sash windows, and composition roofing. Signs for POTTERY, POTTERY AND FIGURINES, INDIAN ART AND SOUVENIRS, ART AND TOURS line the pueblo roads. Almost as apparent are the dogs. Dozens of them, mostly mongrels, lie against the buildings or prowl the close streets. A satellite dish, positioned just off the central plaza, is evidence that the Indians have one foot in the twenty-first century.

On feast days the character of Santa Clara changes drastically. The ordinarily quiet pueblo is suddenly inundated with outsiders. Relatives return to renew their ties; tourists arrive in rented cars and in huge tour buses; Indians travel from the Navajo and Hopi reservations and often from as far away as North Dakota and Canada. There is a tackiness to aspects of the gathering that mysteriously preserves its underlying holiness. Stands selling sno-cones and corn dogs and cotton candy compete with those featuring fry bread and burgers and Indian tacos; artists lay out their wares. Grease sizzles on grills and bubbles in deep vats. While the carnival churns on at the edge of the central village and traders do a brisk business in the booths of the bazaar, gloriously costumed dancers climb out of the kiva and descend the steps into the plaza. The ponderous drums fill the streets of the pueblo. The dances begin.

People flock to various pueblo homes to eat. Friends and relatives gather. Very often complete strangers show up, sunburned and self-conscious Anglos no one knows, invited by people who haven't bothered to come themselves. Santa Clara people take it all in stride. They feed their guests in shifts, seating those waiting for table space in their living room or outside in the shade of a porch; they keep the dining chairs full, the whole thing done in a relaxed atmosphere. There is a formality about the feast, with place settings and a plethora of food. The hosts pass *posole* and chile and beans and ham and turkey and *chicos* and salad and Jell-O and pour cup after cup of Kool-Aid and coffee until everyone has eaten. When you thank them, they tell you they are blessed to have been able to feed so many hungry people.

Dogs, near El Rancho

To the Indians who live in the pueblo and belong there, the village is holy; it is holy in a way few outside visitors would understand. No matter how it has been circumscribed and whittled down by the denial of old treaties and further carved into by legal voodoo on the part of the U.S. government, what land the Indians have managed to hold on to is sacred to them.

"The pueblo, this land, has always been the one constant in my life," says the Santa Clara artist Rosemary Lonewolf.

Rosemary is a beautiful woman. She dresses in a style appropriate to the moment; at one of her exhibitions in New York City or Beverly Hills she might put on a traditional beaded buckskin dress and heirloom jewelry; today, in the pueblo, she wears designer jeans and a soft pink cotton shirt. Her long, dark hair, pulled back and fastened with a beaded comb, glistens. Her features have a gentle radiance. Her strong sense of self, her talent as an artist, and her awareness of her Indian heritage have allowed her a unique worldview. However, being in the pueblo and of the pueblo is the most important aspect of her life.

"I wasn't born here," she explains. "My dad was, though. My grandfather assisted my grandmother in the births of all their children, and they were born right here on the pueblo. I envy that. I was born in some godforsaken place in Arkansas. My dad was in the army at the time. We came back to the pueblo after a few months. We always came back. Where else would we go? This was home. The pueblo is home to most Indians—even if they live off the pueblo. Santa Clara is the one thing that never changes. People come and go in your life, but the land—this place—is always there." She stops to laugh at herself. "I sound like Scarlett O'Hara in *Gone With the Wind*."

We sit in the living room of her home, a small government house located away from the old pueblo. This is the hour in the afternoon when the winds of late spring begin to blow, the beginning of the hot time before the summer rains. From the window, I watch a dust devil rise up and go swirling along the dirt street. Everywhere is a withering dryness. One feels it and tastes it. Only the cholla cactus stand out, their spiny arms sprouting red blossoms.

In many ways, Rosemary's home could be a middle-class home anywhere. Here are the ordinary couches, curtains, coffee table, and accoutrements one might see in a typical American home in Iowa or Washington; even the plants are the same—the potted ficus, the Norway pine, the succulents. There the similarity ends: Rosemary's collection of superb Indian art takes up every inch of available wall space. It includes a few traditional elements: a beautifully crafted cradleboard, with feathers tucked in bands that once held her baby, hangs on one wall; a pair of beaded moccasins is suspended from a nail high on the opposite wall. Pieces of her own pottery are displayed alongside examples of the work of her family and friends. Her pots are small, but their scale is deceptive. They are elaborately and painstakingly carved and show her exceptional talent in drawing and design as well as her extraordinary use of color, which is at once strong and unmistakably feminine.

The sense of place, of Santa Clara, this small part of the earth, her roots, is on Rosemary's mind. "I can't make a move here without being reminded of my heritage. I was out gardening today and found myself turning things up in the yard—arrowheads and pot shards. They tell me that I am just one more person in a long chain of people. The chain may be broken tomorrow—Los Alamos may explode and take us all with it—but I know that even if the rest of the world breaks away, the pueblo will always be here. It is that strong.

"I travel and do business outside of the pueblo and I really enjoy seeing the cities and doing those different things. But on the way back to the pueblo, coming over the opera hill north of Santa Fe, especially in the morning light, I think, Boy, am I glad I live here. People don't realize how special this place is. I hope they never do. I feel protective about it. The only people I want to welcome here are the ones who won't pave everything over and put up those ugly two- and three-story buildings."

She senses this uniqueness not exclusively in the Pueblo land but also in her connection to it. "My work is so much a part of my pueblo that I can't consider living anyplace else for any length of time. It includes the clay I use and the special prayers I have been taught to say while I get the clay and while I work with it."

Part of Rosemary's appreciation has come from time spent away from Santa Clara. When she was a child, her family lived in Colorado Springs and came back to the pueblo only for long weekends, vacations, and feast days. This was before the fame of her father, the artist Joseph Lonewolf, was firmly established.

"We were dancing for the tourists up there," she says with a grimace. "That almost became a family tradition. For at least three generations we have danced for tourists. My dad did it, and his dad. When I was first married, that's what my husband and I were doing. Paul was beating the drum and Rose, six months pregnant," she says, pointing to herself, "was dancing. I remember thinking, Man, this can't be it. There's got to be more to life than this. About that time, my dad was injured at work and we decided to move back to the pueblo. It was a forced retirement for him. And thank goodness for the housing project. It gave us a place here to live."

She becomes silent. Again, I hear the wind gusting. A newspaper cartwheels across the next lot and then lodges against the fence.

Rosemary's education in the traditional arts came at the hands of her family. She began working while she was a child, as many Indians do, picking up clay and imitating her elders. She learned from her grandfather, her father, and her aunt, each of whom has a strong and distinctive style. She claims it came, too, from a much deeper source, from the very soul of the pueblo; she is convinced that her talent and drive are present in her genes.

"Relatives of mine who were potters go back for generations," she says. "When I go to Puye, to the cliffs south of here, and I see a shard uncovered by the rain or the wind I get this indescribable feeling. I know that the person who made that ancient pot was probably related to me."

Puye is a spectacular ruin that was inhabited by the Santa Clara ancestors centuries ago. The cliff face is honeycombed with dwellings, and a ruined village sits atop Santa Clara Canyon, a few miles southwest of Rosemary's house.

I ask what made her decide finally to turn pottery-making into a full-time profession.

"That isn't a decision you make," she says. "My dad and my grandfather taught me that if you are chosen, then you will work with clay. And I believe that. It is not something you choose to do. You are chosen, and being selected is an honor. You learn that if you have the talent you don't abuse it and you don't waste it. There are prayers you say and certain other things you do to protect your talent. Working is almost ceremonial.

You don't do anything to abuse your power to create or that power might be taken away. That's the way it has always been for us."

I am curious about her insistence on a connection with tradition, with the ancient, the tribal. "Your pots are not strictly imitative of that old world."

"No . . ." She smiles, as though she had expected the question. "I live in this world. Pots are no longer used as they were then—not to cook in or to hold water. We cook in metal. We've got Tupperware," she says, making a joke. "I didn't grow up in that ancient tradition. Even my dad's pots are purely art pieces. My own became that. If people ask me why they aren't functional, I ask them how they use the paintings they own. Do they cook in them or mix their martinis in them? It's strange that people believe a pot has to be used as a pot—I mean in the old way."

"How do you explain the nontraditional elements in your work?"

"I don't," she says kiddingly. "Many of the subjects I choose to put in my work are drawn directly from the culture, even though they look very modern—like butterflies, which are important to the pollination process, and animals, which figure into the animal dances. Although I draw them more realistically, my designs relate back to the earlier people, even to the Mimbres potters of twenty-five centuries ago."

"What's the connection? Is it the story?"

"Not just the story, which is important to me, of course. It's the repetition of images and the way they relate that are absolutely traditional. I've worked with female themes, sexual themes—pregnancy, marriage, love, the birth process. I've used corn and water, cats, mice, fish, and a lot of other symbols I've drawn from the ancients to tell my stories. Each of these experiences is significant in my life."

Rosemary's first marriage to the artist Paul Speckled Rock ended in divorce. With the divorce came the problem of courtship. She was gaining notoriety for her own works of art and she had her life in the pueblo; but there was also her professional life beyond the pueblo. She had brought the two worlds into balance within herself, but it was difficult to meet a man of that same mind.

"I met a lot of Indian men who were considered eligible bachelors." She rolls her eyes at the term. "But as men most of them were really only effective in the pueblo. When I took them to activities and art shows on the outside most of them were totally immobilized. I mean, there were things I could trust my sixteen-year-old son to do that these guys couldn't handle—something as simple as checking out of a hotel and making reservations for rooms in another city. Day-to-day things you have to do to survive on the road. They couldn't do them.

"I tried relationships with Anglo men. In some ways it was better, in others it was disastrous. Most of them just couldn't understand Indian ways. It's more complicated than a Catholic trying to understand a Baptist. When the pueblo was shut off because of a ceremony and I said I had to get home before a certain hour, they would say, 'Yeah, sure. I've heard that line before.' With an Indian, I'd never have had to explain that. It's like being with someone who has the same religion, the same beliefs."

There was an exception. "Once," she says, "an Anglo guy from Texas almost convinced me to move off the pueblo. We got so serious, in fact, that he drove over one weekend, prepared to move me to Texas. It was the weekend of the deer dance. I went up to watch the deer come down off the hill in the early hours of the morning and all of a sudden it hit me: *Rose, this is what you are leaving.* It wasn't only my family. It was everything I was. I felt like I was literally being torn away from it. And I couldn't do it. I had to send him away, alone. I was where I wanted to live and I knew how strongly the pueblo was connected to my life and my work.

"It hit me again with another Anglo guy who'd been born in Los Alamos and raised here in the valley. He had never been involved with anyone outside of his ethnic group before, but he was open-minded, appreciative of the Indian culture and supportive of me. One night I told him that when I go down to a dance it is like being in church. Well, he couldn't understand that. It didn't fit with his idea of church. Like most Anglos, he didn't think of the dances as prayers. I realized then that spiritually we were miles apart." She spreads her hands and sighs.

"Again, the culture won. It is that strong. Which is something I've been trying to teach to my son, Adam. One Easter when I was going to dance, I told him: 'You're coming down into the kiva tonight.' He wasn't going to dance. But he came down anyway. This usually happens when kids are young. They need to be with somebody because the kiva is pretty intimidating. You get a bunch of old-timers in there and they can be frightening. But he went and now, hopefully, if he wants to go in he can do it on his own."

"Does he have a desire to participate?" I ask.

"Oh, yes. I wanted him to begin dancing, so I organized a family dance. Which is not the same as putting together a birthday party or a barbecue. It takes so much planning and work. I mean, it took a few years. I went to my uncle and asked what I needed to do to have a buffalo dance. He said I had to find people who could drum. I needed another dancer, a male dancer, because they actually lead the dance. I had danced the dance before, but being a woman I knew only what a woman does. I had to find a man who could show Adam the steps and who'd be free at Christmastime to perform it with him. One of my younger cousins said he would do it. His sister wanted to dance, too. Because they were in the family, that made it even better. It brought the family closer.

"The dance had to begin in one of the homes in the main village. My aunt Grace Medicine Flower was the only one with a home in the village that had enough room. I went to her and she gave me permission to use her house.

"Then I had to get together the costumes. Moccasins had to be made. Feathers had to be gotten. When you dance from house to house, people from the different homes give you gifts. So I needed young boys to go around with us and collect those gifts. There had to be someone to watch for any parts of the costumes that might come loose or fall off during the dance. These became the jobs of my cousins.

"Finally, we had everything prepared and we danced. That was the easy part. And it went quickly. When we got back home that night, Adam said, 'When do we dance again?'"

Frustrated by the men she'd met, Rose, who admits to being impulsive, decided to place an ad in the singles column of a newspaper.

"I wouldn't say I was getting desperate," she smiles, "but I figured that out there somewhere had to be a single male Indian who was also tired of the usual dating scene, the hanging out in bars. I wrote up my want list: a man of Indian descent who respected his traditional values but who was also comfortable in the contemporary world. A non-smoker, a moderate drinker. I explained who I was so they would have some idea of what they were getting into. In more ways than one." She raises her eyebrows.

In spite of her request for an Indian male, her first two responses came from Anglos. "One was a teacher who worked with Indians—which was a common ground. We went out once but nothing sparked. Next was this weird psychic, one of the healy-feelies of Santa Fe. He was not so much interested in me as in using me to get at Indian traditional methods."

Adam, now a teenager, comes in from school with two friends. The wind snatches the screen door out of his hand and slaps it back against the side of the house. He looks sheepish for a second, then he and his friends lumber single-file back to his room. His door closes and the thump-thump of the bass on a rock-and-roll tape begins vibrating through the walls.

"It wasn't until I went through another relationship with an Anglo that I realized how important it was to share a cultural base. I had seen too many relationships go bad, including my own parents' marriage. I didn't have the emotional strength for that.

"Oddly enough, the same day my relationship with that Anglo guy ended I went down into the kiva and met Lewis." She becomes more animated now, reflecting how her world suddenly came alive with this new man. "During the dance practice period is when we had our first date. I had known Lewis for years, but either I was in a relationship or he was in a relationship and we were never free to connect. Lewis told me later that he had read my singles ad in the paper and had been interested but he was seeing someone else. At the time we finally got together, I guess it was because all the stars were finally right. Everything just fell into place."

Lewis Baca ended Rose's years of searching. He, too, had been married and had one child. He came from a traditional background; his parents lived in Santa Clara. A graphic artist working in Albuquerque for Intel, the computer-chip company, he had the ability to maintain his Native American heritage and function in the world outside of the pueblo.

Everything began to fall into place for a wedding blessed with all the intricacies of Indian traditional ceremony. Then a sudden complication cropped up.

"Ever since I was a child I've had this desire to go to China," Rose says. She can trace her interest back to a cistern they had in the backyard. "The top on the cistern kept sinking in and my mom told us that if we dug it out we'd reach China, which she said was on the other side of the world. China! That image started to grow in my mind. In high school my advanced history course spent one semester studying China. Those months of study fed the spark. I was disappointed to find out that you couldn't visit China. It was as far away as the moon. Then Richard Nixon opened up relations with China. One of my collectors went over and brought back a couple of little fans for Adam. They were tinder for the fire. Something in my blood kept saying: *Go! Find a way.*"

The idea of the land bridge to Asia, and possible cultural ties between the peoples of the continents, increased her desire to go. In some ways her longing to visit Asia was similar to the bond she felt with the ancient souls in her ancestral Puye. There was a strength in it she felt difficult to explain—even to herself.

"A girlfriend sent me a package of information concerning a group headed to China. That particular trip didn't pan out, but the same organization was hosting a women's-issues conference in China a few months later. They invited me to serve on a panel made up of minorities. I was on my way.

"By that time Lewis and I were engaged. We had set our wedding date for October. When we found out I was going to China for sure, Lewis said, 'Boy, I think you need someone to carry your luggage.' We laughed about it, but we got busy and found funding for Lewis to go and document the trip. It worked out perfectly."

"You'd had this trip in your mind for so many years, what was your reaction when you finally arrived in China?"

"We landed in Shanghai at night. My first impression was of the intense humidity and the smell of coal, which they burn throughout China. It reminded me of New York City, but it wasn't as noisy. I suppose if we had landed in daylight my impression would have been entirely different. What I remember from later are the beautiful rural landscapes and the huge crowds. You get used to the crowds. Unlike crowds in New York City, where you are just lost, in China people give you your space—even in crowds.

"Because this particular group I was with was concerned with children's health and welfare I wasn't able to see as many artists as I wanted. But I did meet a few and I filed their names away for future reference. The place where I finally spoke directly to artists was in Tibet. These were Chinese painters who taught at the Tibetan University. Right away they were interested in how much money the artworks they were trying to sell would bring in the United States."

The music in Adam's bedroom stops abruptly. The three teenage boys shuffle into the living room. Rose sends them to Espanola for hamburgers so we can continue talking.

"When did you decide China might be a great place to get married?"

"The evening Lewis knew he had funding to go he said, 'Rose, you know what I've been thinking?' And I said, 'Stop, Lewis, I know what you're going to say and I've already thought of it.' We were both thinking it would be neat to get married in China. The next day I called our sponsor who said the doors were pretty much closed. One of us had to be Chinese before they would consider it."

Rose persisted. "Once we arrived in San Francisco for a day of orientation, the president of this organization said she had been speaking to some people and a wedding might be possible in the American Embassy in Beijing. We might have been happy with that, but we kept pushing for something more traditional.

"After our Chinese guide found out we wanted to get married, things started falling in place. It's one of those situations where you know the hand of God has to be in it.

"We knew a wedding ceremony in China was a problem, but the closer we got to Tibet the more possible it seemed that we'd be able to do it there. Though Tibet is a part of China, they weren't under the government eye so much. They could look the other way.

"Still, there was so much red tape and hassle I figured we'd end up getting married in the embassy or in Japan. Lewis said, 'No, Rose, wait and see. It'll happen.'

"The guides had told us to take only one suitcase to Tibet. Lewis was so confident he packed his Indian ribbon shirt, which he had planned to wear during the ceremony here. But I left my good clothes, my heels and dresses in the hotel in Chengdu and took only jeans and T-shirts to Tibet.

"Our plane landed in Tibet just after sunrise and the country had that early-morning feeling. I remember how crisp and clear the sky was—so bright. While we were waiting for the luggage, I kept thinking how much the landscape looked like New Mexico, particularly our area here in the north."

ESPANOLA

Rose felt an incredible sense of kinship with the people and the country. She saw many similarities between New Mexico and Tibet. The landscape was the beginning; but the people were the real key. "The faces of the people looked so familiar. That's the only word for it—familiar. They were Indian faces. The women wore turquoise and lots of coral and silver. That, combined with their appearance, the shape of their faces, gave them a real similarity to our Pueblo women, or the Navajos. The homes were like ours—adobe and stone—with vigas, architecture similar to ours. One of the things I noticed in the market and bought right away was a woven belt. The designs looked Indian. I thought, How did this Tewa woven belt make it to Tibet?

"We were pretty certain now that the wedding would happen," she says. "But there were still a couple of wrinkles. In the morning, speaking with the Chinese and the local Tibetans, we would agree on something; then it had to be discussed behind the scenes with the big guys. The guide would come back at lunch and say, 'Okay we can do this.'" She mimics his sawing hand gesture. "It was decided that we would follow the Tibetan procedure for choosing the right day to get married, based on our birthdays. The guide told us we would have to consult a monk to determine the best day out of the entire year. I thought, Well, that blows it because we are only here for four days."

Following a Jeep trip in search of the monk, banging through potholes, racing up and down the narrow streets of the town, they discovered he was at their own hotel, the Holiday Inn in Lhasa. "We went into his office, a room made over in the Tibetan style, with cushions and tapestries and burning incense. The monk held regular office hours there to counsel people on herbal medicine and give treatments. The translators told him we needed an auspicious day for a marriage. The monk pulled out these tablets, flipped through the pages, and made a few notes. From then on everything was said in Tibetan. We worried that no date within our time period would be good for us. The guide said there were things you could do to counter such bad omens.

"Finally the monk wrote down the date. The guides gave the thumbs-up sign. They had the biggest grins on their faces. The best day was the last day we'd be in Tibet. Heading back to the elevators to our room we asked the guides, 'How did he know this was the good day?' They said that for me, for a woman—then they giggled and blushed and couldn't go on. The Chinese guide stepped in and said, 'It's just that a woman needs to be more receptive to a man on the wedding day and for Rosemary this is the best day.' Lewis said, 'What about me? Is it the best day for me?' She said, 'Not the best date — but second-best date.'

"The Tibetan wedding our guide described was similar to an Indian celebration. Our cultures were so close. There isn't any set ceremony like Anglo people have in their churches. On a certain day two people join their lives. Which is pretty much what happens in our Indian culture, with the families serving as witnesses. Afterward, there is a big feast.

"As soon as I was sure it was going to happen in Tibet," she says, laughing, "my first thought was, 'Rose, you're gonna have to get married in jeans and a T-shirt.' I guess it happened that way so I'd be forced to hunt for a wedding dress." Then she adds, "I believe in those things.

"In the market, we were hit by this throng of Tibetans selling their goods. Earlier, we'd been introduced to two of the women. One spoke just enough English to ask what I wanted. I touched her blouse. She looked down, puzzled. Finally, through sign language, pidgin English, and a couple of words I dug out of the dictionary, I made her understand. She hurried me past the first couple of stalls we went to and guided us up an alley. The farther we got away from the heart of the market, the cheaper the prices became.

"Eventually I saw what I wanted, a really nice embroidered, woven silk skirt. It was green, shot through with gold threads and had an embossed look to it. I was ready to pay the first price they asked. I felt it was more than reasonable. But no, our Tibetan friend bargained, brought the price down, and we bought it.

"Then off we went looking for a blouse. Through hand gestures I made her understand I wanted a wraparound style, with no buttons. We found a blouse in a bright sun-gold color to match the colors in the skirt. The woman in the shop folded it into itself in a very strange way. I keep it folded like that even now so I will remember it. We bought aprons and prayer scarves to complete the outfit.

"All the time we were walking from booth to booth, women following us kept pulling out necklaces and bracelets they wanted to sell. We kept laughing and saying no. After going all the way around the market we ended up buying one small coral necklace with an amber stone suspended from it and a string of coral.

"In my backpack I had some Plains Indian jewelry an Oto woman had made for me. They kept showing me all their jewelry and I thought, I'm going to show them my jewelry. I pulled it out and the woman who'd been showing us around gasped. Immediately everyone in the market knew about my necklace. They crowded around. Lewis took a photograph of it. I know I am in the center of the picture, but you can't see me. Our woman sized up the crowd, put the necklace in its case, and slipped it into my backpack. Then she gave them all a look that said *Beat it!* And they cleared out."

"What was it about your necklace that attracted them?"

"Probably the same thing that excited me about their jewelry," she says. "The same thing I'd seen in the belt I'd bought. They recognized a connection, as though somewhere in the distant past the designs had come from the same place."

"You mentioned the monk had worked out times for the wedding," I say. "What were they?"

"He told us there were two best times on this particular day to join our lives. The best time for our private ceremony was two o'clock. We would say whatever we planned to say to each other. That was the real ceremony. We planned a public ceremony for later in the evening."

With all the preparations, the language barrier, and their efforts to get the wedding to happen, neither Rose nor Lewis had given serious thought to where it would take place.

"Some people suggested there was a nice garden in the Holiday Inn grounds." Rose makes a sour face. "That didn't feel right at all. We showed a taxi driver a postcard of an open area with a view of the Potala Palace in the background. He took us to a park that was perfect. We found a spot along the highway for our private ceremony, a little point that jutted out into the Lhasa River, with prayer flags and this incredible view.

"The day of the wedding, during lunch, Lewis and I slipped away alone." The memory renders her voice softer, her descriptions become more lyrical. "As it happens here

DANCERS, SAN ILDEFONSO

in New Mexico, in Tibet there is usually a little summer afternoon thunderstorm. We went to the point we had visited the night before. A storm was gathering, all these beautiful thunderclouds moving gradually up the river. It was starting to rain. The prayer flags made it a holy and sacred site. We understood the significance of the flags. In our own native religion we have sacred sites marked out in different ways. As long as our backs were to the highway we could see only the magnificent mountains and the river. It was perfect. Lewis had brought cornmeal, which we use in our ceremonies. We threw our cornmeal and asked for a blessing. We said how we felt about each other and what we expected from each other. It was special. For me, that was the moment I was truly married."

"After the drama of your private vows, didn't the public ceremony seem anticlimactic?"

"Well, at first it was kind of awkward," she says. "Our group from the States felt they had to sing 'Here Comes the Bride.' We told them we had been drawn to this place for a special reason, and we felt they were intended to be part of it. It's the same when we dance in the pueblo. In our beliefs, outside people who discover one of our dances, not really expecting to see anything, are brought to it to receive its blessings. We explained to the group that we felt that was why they were there.

"Once the ceremony started and the Tibetans saw people putting prayer scarves on us they knew something important was going on. They crowded around, too.

"We had explained to our group that in our ceremonies guests could give advice to the couple. So they read poems or scripture or talked. Another custom is that instead of a maid of honor or a best man, Indian couples choose a married couple to serve as their examples. The only married couple was our delegation leader and his wife, and she happened to be Navajo. They were our proxies.

"Rather than exchanging rings, Lewis and I exchanged two stones that we had asked a local carver to inscribe with our vows in Tibetan, which were a definition of what love means to us. Tibetan reads from left to right, just like English, so when the two stones are joined you can read it—providing you can read Tibetan." She hands me the stones.

"Our feast was held at a Tibetan restaurant," Rose goes on. "Originally it was planned as a special dinner for our group, but after we knew the wedding would happen the arrangements were changed to include some traditional elements of a Tibetan wedding dinner. The whole staff of the restaurant was waiting outside and they each presented us with a prayer scarf. We sat in front of an altar. On our table was a container filled with what looked like ground flour formed into a mound, with sheaves of wheat stuck in it. Waiters brought in containers of holy water. We were told to dip our ring fingers into the water and sprinkle the drops on the crowd three times as a blessing. They brought in a dish with a kind of sweet rice and berries or raisins in it. We ate three bites. Next came a barley wine, kind of cloudy like watered-down milk. It tasted good. We took three sips and on the third one had to down it to the bottom. That was a little rough.

"Then a waiter brought a dish molded like a ram. It looked meaty, like liverwurst. I was prepared for a livery taste. But it was a dish made from some kind of flour. They cut off the head of the ram and presented it to a picture of the Dalai Lama on the altar where we were seated.

"The high point for me was when three monks danced for us, which is usually done in honor of the Dalai Lama. In some ways it was like a kachina dance I had seen at Hopi, although this was more vigorous. We knew it was a ceremonial dance. So beautiful." She shakes her head.

"Chinese and Tibetan beer was flowing for everyone in the restaurant. Most of our ladies were a little too proper to drink much, but our bus driver took advantage of the free beer—so we had one wild ride back to the hotel. Fortunately at one o'clock in the morning there is not a traffic problem in Lhasa.

"Early the next morning, I watched Lewis packing all the prayer scarves people had given us, doing the old sitting-on-the-suitcase routine to get it to lock, and I said, 'Don't tell me you're going to take all those back with us?' And he said 'Yeah, just think of it. We can get them out at our own reception and blessing later.' We also had two embroidered silk scarves that we'd bought at the Potala Palace. We had given those to each other in the ceremony. Jokingly, Lewis said, 'When the Dalai Lama comes to Santa Fe, we can always present him with these.'"

The Dalai Lama *did* come to Santa Fe, less than a year later. "We were getting ready to go to this special audience he was having for Indian people. So we got down the prayer scarves. First Lewis was a little reluctant to take both of them. I said, 'Lewis, you brought those all the way back from Lhasa and you told me that you wanted to give them to the Dalai Lama. Now I'm going to hold you to it.' Finally, he agreed.

"At first, they weren't going to let us give any gifts to him. Apparently the other gifts were scheduled gifts from the various pueblos, although one little girl did get up and give him her teddy bear." Rose's determination surfaced as soon as she saw there was an obstacle. "I said to Lewis, 'I don't care what happens, we're giving him the scarves.' Nobody stopped us. We got in line. Lewis had brought one of our wedding photos. And when we presented him with the scarves, Lewis took the microphone and explained what had happened in Tibet. Then he turned around and showed the Dalai Lama the wedding photograph. Twice the Dalai Lama repeated, 'How beautiful, how beautiful.'"

This was a powerful moment for Rose, and now she sits quietly. "After we gave him the prayer scarves, he motioned to his translator and the man came over and presented us with two of the Dalai Lama's prayer scarves. So we still have prayer scarves, but these are even more special. At that instant, I had this overwhelming feeling that every-thing had come full circle. Everything was complete. It was not coincidence or anything else. It's just the way things were meant to be."

We sit quietly, listening to the wind. Rosemary has woven together the magic of the cultures in a mesmerizing way. The story of their marriage has the overtones of a story-book tale. It could have been the high point in anyone's life. For her it was the fulfillment of two dreams. Like her pottery, her talent, it came from something deeper, something as profound as her Native American heritage. She will always believe the hand of God was behind it. The hand of some god.

Rosemary sees me to the door. A gust of wind brings a dried tumbleweed swirling onto the porch. I mention how strong the wind is. Rosemary smiles. "It's just like Grandpa always says: 'There are so many evil people in the world and the wind is just trying to blow them away.'"

Saturday Afternoon, Espanola

El Abuelo, Los Matachines de Alcalde